Rail freight since 1968

COAL

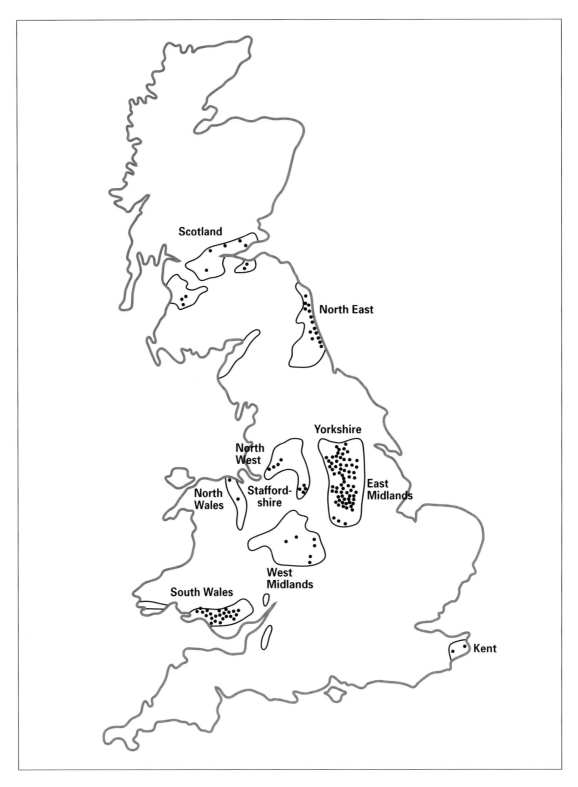

UK coalfields with approximate locations of deep mines open in 1984.

Rail freight since 1968

COAL

Paul Shannon

·RAILWAY HERITAGE·
from
The NOSTALGIA Collection

First published in 2006

British Library Cataloguing in Publication Data

A catalogue record for this book is available from the British Library.

ISBN 1 85794 263 9
ISBN 978 1 85794 263 7

Silver Link Publishing Ltd
The Trundle
Ringstead Road
Great Addington
Kettering
Northants NN14 4BW

Tel/Fax: 01536 330588
email: sales@nostalgiacollection.com
Website: www.nostalgiacollection.com

Printed and bound in Great Britain

All photographs are by the author unless otherwise credited.

Half title Nos 20088 and 20137 haul a rake of empty HEA hoppers out of Toton Old Bank sidings just before sunset on 17 July 1989.

Below No 58043 propels its train under the rapid loader at Bagworth before working an mgr service to Willington power station on 30 October 1986. Coal loading at Bagworth ceased around 1990 when reserves became worked out.

A Silver Link book
from
The NOSTALGIA *Collection*

Contents

Preface

The last four decades have seen momentous changes both on the railway and in the coal industry. In 1968 'merry-go-round' trains, with their potential for on-the-move loading and discharge, were just beginning to usher in a new era in the movement of coal by rail. But many other coal trains at that time still consisted of strings of loose-coupled wagons, requiring time-consuming marshalling and with manual discharge at hundreds of receiving points throughout the country. The coal industry itself was still a major player in the British economy and even had enough capacity to export to mainland Europe. As for consumers, coal was still an important fuel in the home and in a range of industries. Those customers without their own siding would often receive coal from a local station goods yard or concentration depot. The use of coal in the electricity supply industry was still growing, but only the newest power stations were equipped for merry-go-round operation, and old-fashioned operations remained elsewhere.

The relentless decline of deep mining in Britain had a profound effect on railway operations, as the number of loading points shrank and as the productivity from most of the survivors grew. A significant proportion of the freight-only route mileage was deleted from the map in areas such as South Wales and North East England. The complex track layouts at pitheads were gradually replaced by simple facilities such as a single loading siding with run-round loop, and at most locations the use of pilot locomotives became unnecessary as the BR train locomotive would stay with its train during loading. The merry-go-round system became every bit as successful as its promoters had hoped, even though it proved unrealistic to build continuous loops at pitheads and other loading points. Meanwhile, old-style coal trains gradually bowed out as customers either adapted to modern wagons or switched to delivery by road.

During the 1990s the pace of change accelerated as the railway, coal and electricity supply industries all passed into the private sector. The opportunities for rival railway companies to compete for coal traffic were limited at first as all three former Trainload Freight divisions – Loadhaul, Mainline Freight and Transrail – were reunited by English, Welsh & Scottish Railway (EWS) and the open access aspirations of National Power were short-lived. However, Freightliner Heavy Haul later challenged the monopoly of EWS and established successful operations on a number of key routes. The tonnage of coal moved by rail fell with the opening of new gas-fired power stations, but in tonne-mileage terms the traffic rose significantly as the English power generators replaced coal from local pits with more distant imported and Scottish opencast sources. By early 2006 most existing coal-fired stations had had flue gas desulphurisation equipment fitted or authorised, which should ensure the survival of many rail-borne coal flows for at least another decade.

This book traces the development of British coal trains from the early days of merry-go-round to the first decade of the 21st century, looking in detail at the main coal sources and destinations in each region and at the decline of traditional domestic coal traffic on the network as a whole. The information has come from a wide range of sources, including personal observation as well as working timetables and other official documents when available. All dates and other details are believed to be correct, but the author and publisher would be pleased to receive any further information from readers with local knowledge.

The author thanks the photographers who supplied the archive material used in this book, and acknowledges the generous help of very many railway employees, rail freight customers and fellow enthusiasts who supplied information, arranged site visits and provided companionship over the last 30 years. Without their assistance, this book would simply not have been possible.

1.

Coal by rail

In 1968 coal was still a major British industry, with some 300 deep mines combining to produce roughly 150 million tonnes of 'black gold' a year. However, significant rationalisation had already taken place. The number of mines in Britain had shrunk from its maximum of 3,200 in the mid-19th century, while the annual output of coal had peaked at 292 million tonnes as early as 1913. On the whole it was the smaller mines that had closed, so that the average output per mine had increased from 96,000 tonnes a year in 1913 to more than 400,000 tonnes a year in 1968.

What did this mean for the railways? Coal and railways had developed side by side in the 19th century, and in some parts of the country the network of railways was defined by the location of pits. The existence of railways had made it possible to move coal economically over long distances, supplying homes, factories, gas works and power stations throughout the country. The closure of many small pits and small-scale receiving terminals after the Second World War worked to the railway's advantage in enabling it to concentrate its resources on the most productive locations.

During the 1960s the relationship between the railways and coal became strengthened by the building of a new generation of power stations, which, because of their size, lent themselves better than ever before to the rail-borne supply of coal. To enable huge tonnages of coal to be moved with maximum efficiency, British Railways worked together with the Central Electricity Generating Board (CEGB) and the National Coal Board (NCB) to produce an entirely new type of train – the 'merry-go-round' (mgr) operation, with its capacity for loading and discharging whole trainloads of coal on the move.

The mgr breakthrough must rank as one of the most significant rail freight developments of the 20th century. BR calculated that a power station taking 5 million tonnes of coal a year, such as West Burton, could now be serviced by about 200 mgr wagons instead of some 2,000 traditional loose-coupled vehicles. The savings in the wagon fleet were compounded by the fact that there was no longer a need for extensive exchange sidings, nor for shunting locomotives at the pithead or power station.

Once the CEGB had commissioned its pioneering mgr installation at West Burton in 1965, the technology spread quickly to other locations, and by the middle of 1971 some 18 power stations were equipped for automated mgr discharge. The track layout at the newly built power stations included a return loop, so that there was no need for the locomotive to be detached from its train before or after discharge. However, it was not practicable to install a loop at most of the existing power stations that were converted for mgr operation – here it was still necessary for the locomotive to run round its train. A few older power stations such as Elland (Yorkshire) and Carmarthen Bay (South Wales) never had mgr facilities installed, and continued to take their coal in loose-coupled or vacuum-braked wagons until they were closed or adapted for road delivery.

In its ideal form, mgr operation involved direct running between pitheads and power stations with no intermediate marshalling or staging. In some areas several loaded journeys were scheduled within a typical 24-hour period. A good example of that aspiration is the following programme from January 1973:

	arr	dep
Milford Sidings		0920
Kellingley colliery	0940	1058
Eggborough power station	1110	1205
Prince of Wales colliery	1227	1338
Eggborough power station	1408	1503
Kellingley colliery	1514	1647
Eggborough power station	1659	1754
Ackton Hall colliery	1822	2000
Ferrybridge power station	2036	2122
Kellingley colliery	2136	2254
Eggborough power station	2306	0001
Hexthorpe colliery	0054	0127
Ferrybridge power station	0252	0338
Milford Sidings	0426	

In practice, schedules as intensive as this example were the exception rather than the norm. The programme had to take account of available time slots at the pithead and power station, of pathing constraints on the main line, and of train crew requirements. Moreover, the CEGB's progress in equipping its power stations for mgr discharge was faster than the NCB's installation of rapid loaders, mainly because of the very large number of collieries that might at some point be required to supply power station coal.

Nevertheless, the mgr innovation was an instant success, bringing a new lease of life to the railway system's long-established staple freight traffic. Between 1965 and 1982 BR acquired a fleet of more than 11,000 mgr hopper wagons; all were of basically similar design, although there were detail differences such as modified axle springs to allow the wagons to run at 60mph instead of 45mph when loaded, and canopies to reduce dust blow-off. As all mgr wagons were equipped with air brakes only, the options for traction in the early years were rather limited; however, this became less of a problem as BR converted more of its locomotives to dual-brake (vacuum and air) operation, including such elderly designs as the Class 76 Woodhead route electrics dating back to 1950.

A sea of empty coal wagons and other rolling-stock occupies Toton East Yard on 13 March 1980. Many will have already made their last revenue-earning journey.

Above Rope-worked inclines were a feature of many industrial railway systems in hilly areas. Unfitted 21-ton hopper wagon No E252605 descends into Whitehaven harbour with coal from Haig Colliery on 20 June 1968. *Michael Mensing*

Below One of the earliest batch of Class 44 'Peaks', No D5 *Cross Fell*, passes Kibworth on the Midland main line with a Toton to Brent (Cricklewood) coal train in April 1968. The Midland was the busiest route into London for coal traffic, with the timetable for 1969 showing roughly one coal train an hour through Wellingborough. *J. H. Cooper-Smith*

Several coal depots in the Sheffield area still received coal in traditional mineral wagons in the early 1980s. A few MCOs stand in the siding at Deepcar as No 76040 heads away from Sheffield with a trans-Pennine coal train on 9 January 1981.

Other industrial users followed the example of the CEGB in installing mgr discharge facilities for coal. Early examples were the NCB export terminals at Immingham and Leith Docks, the British Steel Corporation at Scunthorpe, Ravenscraig and Redcar, Bowaters at Sittingbourne (Ridham Dock), Associated Portland Cement at Northfleet, Tunnel Cement at Tring, and Aberthaw Cement at Aberthaw. However, the costs of installing mgr discharge at these locations were substantial and in recent years a number of coal customers have shunned potential mgr operation in favour of grab discharge from flat-bottomed wagons.

Despite the widespread introduction of the mgr system, BR continued to run loose-coupled coal trains into the 1980s and vacuum-braked trains until the early 1990s. On the whole, antiquated practices lasted longest where there were short-distance self-contained flows, such as from the South Wales valleys to nearby ports. But the traditional wagonload network also continued to convey household coal in vacuum-braked wagons until 1984, one year after BR had transferred most other less-than-trainload flows to the air-braked Speedlink network.

While the number of deep mines had already shrunk from around 1,100 in 1947 – the year in which the NCB was formed – to just 293 in 1970, the programme of pit closures continued unabated in the 1970s and 1980s. The year-long miners' strike of 1984/85, triggered by the NCB's proposal to close Cortonwood colliery near Barnsley, hastened the closure programme: 23 pits were lost in 1985, 17 in 1986, and 34 more by the end of the decade. Nearly all these mines had been rail-connected and their collective closure brought the demise of numerous freight-only branch lines as well as colliery sidings and yards.

Taking a longer-term view, scarcely a year between 1970 and 2004 passed without the closure of one or more deep mines. By summer 2005 just nine deep mines remained in operation, of which eight were owned by UK Coal, the company originally known as RJB Mining, which took over most former NCB mines in England. The ninth pit, Tower in South Wales, was the only independently owned mine to survive, following the closure of Hatfield colliery near Doncaster in early 2004.

However, the contraction of the British coal industry did not in itself bring a reduction in rail-borne coal traffic. Some of the lost coal from deep mines was replaced by opencast coal, the annual output of which rose from just 7.3 million tonnes in the 1960s to a peak of 18.6 million tonnes in 1991. Most opencast sites have a shorter life expectancy than deep mines, but in many cases it has been financially viable to provide rail loading facilities within easy reach of the site. In some instances the use of rail is a condition of planning permission.

Those opencast railheads that opened up to the 1980s, such as Maryport (Cumbria) and Coalfields

Above Although BR had used containers to carry coke from Derwenthaugh to Wakefield as early as 1969, it was not until the 1980s that containerised coal found its niche in the domestic and export distribution market. One advantage of using containers was that the coal was handled less and therefore remained in better condition. At Seaforth, on 30 October 1992, a reach stacker owned by the Mersey Docks & Harbour Board lifts a container loaded with Welsh anthracite for export to Northern Ireland.

Right The challenge with any wagonload freight network is to ensure viable loadings on trunk trains and trip workings. A single empty HEA forms 6G30, the 1209 Birkenhead to Washwood Heath service, pictured near Stableford on 18 February 1991. The traction is No 37239, a member of the diminishing pool of Class 37s allocated to Cardiff Canton for Speedlink Coal duties.

Right A contrast of old and new at Silverdale on 5 January 1987: No 47333 pauses in the loop with the 6T55 trip working from Holditch to Crewe, conveying industrial coal for Llanwern in MDV and HTV wagons, while an mgr train passes under Silverdale's rapid loader.

Farm (Leicestershire), tended to be equipped with rapid loading bunkers, but more recent facilities such as Hunslet (Leeds) and Swains Park (Leicestershire) have comprised a simple siding with adjacent hard-standing for loading by mechanical grab. One short-lived loading point in South Wales, at Brynteg on the Onllwyn branch, consisted of nothing more than a small area of flattened ground beside the running line. The overall carryings from opencast sites declined in the late 1990s, mainly as a consequence of planning restrictions.

The second factor mitigating the loss of deep-mined coal traffic has been the phenomenal rise in coal imports. Up to the 1960s, Britain was a net exporter of coal and the level of imports was negligible. The first signs of a turnaround came in the late 1970s, when the British Steel Corporation started to look overseas for its supplies of coking coal. Unlike many other industries, the steel industry could not switch to other fuels because coal and coke are an integral part of its process. By the late 1980s the steel plants at Scunthorpe, Ravenscraig and Llanwern were taking the bulk of their coal from import terminals at Immingham, Hunterston and Port Talbot respectively.

More recently, steam coal for use in power stations has been imported from countries such as Colombia, South Africa, Poland, Russia and Australia, where production costs are much lower than in British deep mines and opencast sites. Furthermore, imported coal generally contains less sulphur than British deep-mined coal, resulting in reduced levels of atmospheric pollution. The volume of imports rose sharply in the 1990s and peaked at 35 million tonnes, which was more than double the total output of Britain's deep mines in 2001.

The railway is well placed to carry imported coal, given that the distances to the end user tend to be great and that the coal has to be transhipped at the port regardless of the onward means of transport. At the time of writing Immingham is the biggest single port of entry for overseas coal, but varying tonnages are also moved from Hull, Redcar, Tyne Dock, Leith, Hunterston, Liverpool, Ellesmere Port, Port Talbot, Newport, Avonmouth and Portbury. Several other ports have been involved in trial or short-term movements, including Grain (Thamesport), New Holland, Invergordon and Glasgow (Rothesay Dock).

While the change to longer-distance flows of imported coal brought additional tonne-mileage for the railway, the total amount of coal consumed in Britain shrank by more than 50% between 1970 and 2000. The losses were particularly acute in the domestic and light industrial sectors, serving homes, schools, hospitals and factories; these were the sectors where coal could easily be replaced by other energy sources. That decline had a profound effect on rail freight in many parts of the country, with numerous industrial coal terminals closing down and with the once ubiquitous station coal yard – already an endangered species in the 1960s – passing into history. One industry that bucked the trend, however, was the cement industry, which increased its rail-borne deliveries of coal in the 1990s.

The electricity supply industry was already the dominant consumer of coal at the start of the period covered by this book. Its dominance continued to increase and by 2002 it accounted for 83% of British coal consumption. However, the electricity supply industry was far from stable during that period. The close relationship between the CEGB and BR, characterised since 1976 by an exclusive 15-year contract, came to an abrupt end in the early 1990s as first the CEGB and then BR passed into the private sector.

The CEGB took on its new form as three public limited companies in January 1991. The coal-fired power stations were divided between National Power and Powergen, while responsibility for power distribution passed to National Grid. Although the railway continued to supply coal to National Power and Powergen, there was no longer the security of a long-term contract. Furthermore, the overall amount of coal declined because of a new entrant to the electricity market – gas.

The so-called 'dash for gas' saw a flurry of new gas-fired power stations come on stream. The proportion of electricity generated from gas in England and Wales rose from almost zero in 1990 to 39% in 2002, while the proportion generated from coal fell from 69% to 32% in the same period. Only the switch to longer-distance coal movements, largely the result of colliery closures as explained above, averted a catastrophic decline in this staple, and traditionally most profitable, sector of rail freight.

The shift from coal to gas hastened the closure of a number of older power stations that used to be fed by rail, including Willington, Blyth, Methil, High Marnham and Drakelow. At the other end of the spectrum, a number of power stations judged to have long-term potential have been fitted with flue gas desulphurisation (fgd) equipment, enabling their owners to comply with the European Large Combustion Plants Directive, which aims to reduce acidification, ground-level ozone and particles throughout Europe by controlling emissions of sulphur dioxide, nitrogen oxides and dust from large combustion plants.

The first station to have fgd fitted was Drax, Britain's largest coal-fired installation, with the capacity to supply 7% of the country's total electricity needs. Other stations with fgd already installed or authorised by 2006 were Ratcliffe, Uskmouth, West Burton, Cottam, Eggborough, Ferrybridge, Fiddlers Ferry, Rugeley and Longannat. The fitting of fgd equipment has not only enhanced the future of rail-borne coal movements – the owner of Drax signed a five-year deal with UK Coal in 2004 – but has also offered the potential for other rail freight flows in the form of inward limestone and outward gypsum.

The privatisation of Trainload Freight in 1994 split BR's merry-go-round coal traffic between three separate administrations: Loadhaul, Mainline and Transrail. The opportunities for competition between the three operators were

Above Coal loading terminals do not come much simpler than this! At Brynteg, a small pad was provided alongside the single-track Onllwyn branch for a short-term flow of reclaimed coal. Coal for Aberthaw is being loaded into HDA wagons at Brynteg on 28 August 1998.

Below An extraordinary survivor in the 21st century: long after most coal concentration depots had closed, the Smallshaws depot at Gobowen was still receiving coal by rail in 2004, for distribution in a large area of Shropshire and North East Wales. The discharge equipment at Gobowen is pictured on 3 April 2005.

limited because traffic flows were allocated on a regional basis, and it was not long before the operators were reunited under EWS ownership. However, some genuine competition arose in 1995 when National Power became a licensed operator and took over some of the coal traffic to Drax power station that would otherwise have gone to Loadhaul. This particular open access operation was short-lived, as EWS took over all National Power's railway assets in 1998.

Longer-term competition for EWS came from the Heavy Haul division of Freightliner, which ran its first trial movements of coal from Teesside to the Aire Valley in December 2000. The company ordered its own fleet of bogie hopper wagons and was soon tendering successfully for a range of traffic flows from Scotland, the East Coast ports and some of UK Coal's remaining pits to power stations in the Aire and Trent valleys.

Another potential open access operator for coal

traffic was Jarvis, reported in 2003 to be planning to buy ten Class 66s and 200 coal hoppers to carry coal from Scotland to Drax. However, the Jarvis proposal became embroiled in controversy because it relied on the availability of paths that EWS and Freightliner claimed not to exist. By late 2005 Jarvis's plans appeared to have been forgotten.

Looking to the future, a study commissioned by the Strategic Rail Authority in 2003 concluded that the market for moving coal to power stations was likely to decline sharply by 2015, with an expected drop in tonne-mileage of between 32% and 58%. The extent of the decline would depend mainly on the ability of coal to compete against gas. The balance between home-produced and imported coal would be likely to shift further in favour of imports, given the high production costs of Britain's deep-mined coal and increasing restrictions on opencast sites. The study noted that several ports would be capable of handling an increase in coal traffic, but those with the best prospects were the deep-water ports of Immingham, Hunterston, Redcar, Port Talbot and Bristol (Avonmouth/Portbury). Already in 2004 Immingham was investing in the second phase of its Humber International Terminal scheme, promising an excellent future for the port, first developed by the Great Central Railway in 1912.

The 2,400MW power station at Longannet forms an imposing backdrop for an arriving coal train, hauled by No 56112, on 13 July 1992. Despite competition from gas, Longannet achieved the highest generation output in its 30-year history in 2000-01, with the coal burn for the year topping 5 million tonnes.

Wagons

The commonest, and simplest, type of coal wagon used in the 1960s was the 16-ton mineral wagon – essentially an open box on wheels, loaded from above and discharged through doors on the sides and at one end. At one time BR operated a fleet of more than 200,000 16-ton minerals; most of them were unfitted and coded MCO for the purposes of BR's Total Operations Processing System (TOPS), but some were fitted with vacuum brakes and coded MCV. Until the 1970s both varieties were a ubiquitous sight in coal yards and in wagonload freight trains, but by the early 1980s the survivors were mainly used on specific trainload flows where provision had not yet been made for more modern stock.

BR also operated a less numerous fleet of 21-ton mineral wagons, built on a 12-foot instead of a 9-foot wheelbase. Again they came in both unfitted and fitted varieties, coded MDO and MDV respectively. The 21-ton minerals were intended for high-volume flows to industrial locations such as power stations, gas works and coking plants. BR also ran a small fleet of 24½-ton mineral wagons, coded MEO, again generally on major industrial flows. The MEOs became extinct in the 1970s, but BR continued to use MDOs and MDVs in some areas, such as South Wales, until the mid-1980s.

Although not specifically designed for coal, some MSV tippler wagons carried loads such as coal slurry to Methil where the use of under-floor hoppers or side doors was not practicable.

The widespread use of hopper wagons for coal had originated on the North Eastern Railway, with its policy of installing staithes wherever coal needed to be unloaded. BR inherited a standard design of steel-bodied hopper wagon from the LNER, with a 21-ton capacity and a 12-foot wheelbase, and built more than 20,000 of its own; these were coded HTO and HTV. In later years the surviving HTVs tended to be used on trainload flows to destinations with hopper discharge facilities but not equipped for mgr wagons, such as Lea Hall (Rugeley). Some HTVs were transferred to sand and stone traffic when no longer required for coal.

A 24½-ton variant of the standard coal hopper, coded HUO, was used on certain flows of power station coal. These unfitted wagons were still being built as late as 1965 and some examples remained in use in the East Midlands until the early 1980s.

For coke traffic, BR operated about 2,000 hoppers with high sides, usually extended by means of wooden planks. They received the code HCO, but only just lasted into the TOPS era.

The merry-go-round revolution was heralded by the introduction of two prototype 32-ton 'HOP32AB' wagons in 1964. Construction of mgr wagons gathered pace in line with the building of new coal-fired power stations, which were their main intended destinations. By 1982 BR had built a fleet of 11,000 mgr hoppers – small compared with the vast numbers of traditional mineral wagons that they replaced, but nonetheless a significant investment by the railway.

Most mgr hoppers were coded HAA when TOPS was introduced. However, the last 460 vehicles were fitted with upgraded suspension to permit a maximum speed of 60mph instead of 45mph when loaded; they were coded HDA. Greater diversification took place in the early 1990s, when further wagons were adapted for 60mph operation when loaded, and some were fitted with canopies to reduce the problem of coal dust blow-off. The fitting of canopies was not new – one of the prototype wagons of 1964 was canopied – but in the early years few colliery screens were high enough to allow their use and they were restricted mainly to Scotland.

By 2001, the mgr wagon fleet consisted of:

2,943	HAA	standard mgr hopper, 45mph loaded and 60mph empty
264	HBA	ex-HDA with canopy
77	HCA	ex-HAA with canopy
161	HDA	mgr hopper with upgraded suspension, 60mph loaded and empty
682	HFA	ex-HAA with aerodynamic canopy
1,228	HMA	ex-HAA with modified brake distributor, 60mph loaded and empty
74	HNA	ex-HFA with modified brake distributor, 60mph loaded and empty

However, some wagons later had their canopies removed in order to prevent damage during loading by mechanical grab; they then reverted to the HAA classification. In 2005 EWS experimented with spraying the coal with a sticky gel as an alternative method of reducing dust blow-off.

For coal traffic to domestic distribution depots and other destinations without mgr door-closing equipment, BR acquired nearly 2,000 air-braked manual-discharge hoppers from 1975 onwards. They were initially coded HBA – a code that was later to be re-used for one of the mgr wagon variants. However, the code was changed to HEA as the wagons were re-sprung for 60mph instead of 45mph operation – a prerequisite for their use on

A selection of traditional coal wagons:
Above MCO B230791 at Biggleswade freight depot on 28 August 1978.

Above MDO B317014 at Whitemoor yard on 13 January 1981. This wagon had been re-bodied at Shildon in 1973.

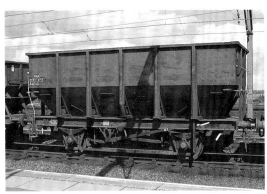

Above left MEO B280762 at Ipswich on 15 October 1980.

Above Re-bodied HTO E289616 at Bristol Wapping Wharf coal depot on 11 September 1977.

Left HUO B337322 at Wolverhampton on 21 August 1979.

Speedlink services. In practice the HBA/HEA wagon fleet was under-utilised as the traffic for which they were intended melted away. Some were used as barrier wagons and others donated their underframes for MEA open box wagons.

Not coal wagons as such, but nevertheless used to carry coal, were two fleets of container-carrying vehicles. BR owned more than 200 30-foot FPA container flats, which were used to carrying Russells containers to Scottish destinations and, later, to places such as Immingham and Hull; many survived in EWS ownership. In 1986 Cawoods introduced its own fleet of 20-foot PFA container flats, dedicated to Northern Irish traffic via Ellesmere Port and, later, Seaforth.

Until the 1980s BR encouraged its coal customers to install hopper discharge facilities; some of those who did not were forced to find an alternative means of transport. That policy changed in the early 1990s, partly because BR recognised that its insistence on using hopper wagons was leading to lost business and partly because of improvements in mechanical grab technology. BR therefore began converting redundant HEA hoppers into MEA open box wagons. EWS carried out further conversions and by 1998 the MEA fleet totalled 573 vehicles. The MEAs were used on various flows of industrial coal, as well as on aggregates traffic. However,

some MEAs were later converted to the lower-sided MFA type for infrastructure traffic.

EWS also introduced a 300-strong fleet of bogie open box wagons, coded MBA. They were destined mainly for aggregates and scrap metal flows but also carried coal from some locations such as Gedling.

National Power provided the first real alternative to the mgr hopper when it introduced its fleet of 85 bogie hopper wagons in 1995/96. Coded JMA, the National Power hoppers were a 75-tonne-capacity design with low-track-force bogies and with bodywork made of a new type of corrosion-resistant steel. The use of bogie wagons instead of two-axle vehicles made it possible to carry a higher tonnage for a given length of train, a useful feature for those locations where the train length was limited by the signalling or track layout.

In December 2000 both EWS and new entrant Freightliner Heavy Haul introduced their own variety of bogie coal wagon, coded HTA and HHA respectively. In all, 1,145 HTAs were built; they would operate in 19-wagon sets with an average payload per train of 1,400 tonnes. The fleet of Freightliner HHAs reached just over 400 vehicles by the end of 2005, operating in sets of either 17 or 19 wagons depending on the terminals served. Both HTAs and HHAs were authorised to run at 75mph empty and 60mph loaded. However, the era of the two-axle mgr wagon was by no means

Coal rolling-stock for the 21st century: EWS No 66182 passes Barnetby on 16 June 2003 with 4Y80, the 0910 empty HTAs from Eggborough to Immingham, while Freightliner Heavy Haul No 66524 calls to pick up empty HHA wagons from the up sidings.

At Tyne Yard on 16 July 2003, the tail lamp is attached to the last HBA wagon on 6S20, the 1220 departure to Falkland.

finished: a number of loading and discharge terminals, including Newport Docks, Uskmouth, Cockenzie and Longannet, were still using exclusively two-axle wagons in the summer of 2005.

Freightliner Heavy Haul

Following Freightliner's management buyout in 1995, the company looked for opportunities to diversify. The first fruits appeared in 1999, when Freightliner won its first contract outside the container-carrying business – a ground-breaking deal to move infrastructure materials for Railtrack – and the Heavy Haul division of Freightliner was born. To cater for the new business, the company ordered 15 Class 66/5 locomotives, which would be delivered between June and November 2000. In the meantime some Class 66/5s belonging to Freightliner Intermodal were made available for Heavy Haul use.

In the summer of 2000 Freightliner Heavy Haul won a contract to move cement for Blue Circle (later Lafarge) from Hope to Dewsbury and Weaste. Then came the coal breakthrough – a contract with Enron to move imported coal to power stations in the Aire valley. For that business FHH had to provide its own wagons, as all existing coal was carried in wagons owned by its competitor, EWS. Its initial order was for 55 102-

tonne glw (gross laden weight) bogie wagons, coded HHA for TOPS purposes, and the first rake entered service on the Redcar to Eggborough flow in December 2000.

An unwelcome hiccough was the collapse of Enron in 2001. However, American Electric Power bought much of Enron's UK interests and continued to put its business on rail. FHH also won contracts with other players in the electricity supply industry, such as British Energy and Drax Power Limited. By 2003 FHH's coal portfolio included deep-mined coal from several pits in Nottinghamshire and Yorkshire, opencast coal from Killoch, Knockshinnoch, New Cumnock and Ravenstruther, and imported coal from Hunterston, Redcar, Immingham and Hull. The destinations were Drax, Eggborough, Ferrybridge, Cottam, West Burton and Rugeley. In 2005 FHH broke the monopoly of EWS on coal movements to Fiddlers Ferry when it introduced a twice-daily service from Ellesmere Port.

FHH also started moving coal from Immingham to the Alcan power station at Lynemouth in 2005 and carried out a number of trials for industrial customers, including Rugby Cement at Foxton and Castle Cement at Clitheroe. For the trials to Rugby and Clitheroe, it used hired two-axle hopper wagons and its own MJA open box wagons respectively.

At the time of writing, FHH covers its

mainstream coal operations with up to 23 sets of 17 HHA wagons. However, some sets are augmented to 19 wagons on routes where the signal spacing and track layout are suitable. The weekly operating schedule is drawn up at FHH's Ferrybridge office, within sight of one of the company's main coal destinations. FHH receives orders from its customers on Monday; it puts together a provisional train plan by Wednesday, and finalises drivers' rosters and, where necessary, lodging arrangements by Friday. But FHH has the flexibility to amend the programme on a day-by-day basis, if for example unforeseen problems at a particular location require trains to be diverted.

Bids for train paths are placed with Network Rail from Tuesday onwards. Where possible FHH uses working timetable paths, but, given the fast-changing pattern of coal flows, many trains run under short-term planning arrangements. FHH keeps its wagons on the move as much as possible and does not need extensive stabling sidings. Routine wagon maintenance is carried out under contract by Marcroft, either at one of the normal FHH stabling locations or at Marcroft's Horbury workshops.

The Class 66/5 traction for FHH coal trains is shared with other FHH flows of cement, aggregates, waste, oil and motor vehicles. FHH appointed London & North Western Railway as its locomotive maintenance contractor in 2002; LNWR officially opened its £1.75 million maintenance depot at Leeds Midland Road in July 2003. The nine-road depot includes a maintenance shed with two pitted roads that can accommodate six locomotives at any one time, together with a fuelling point with two roads, one of which is covered and pitted. However, it is rare to see more than a handful of locomotives at Midland Road at any one time, given that FHH uses its fleet on revenue-earning duties as intensively as possible.

A visit to Ferrybridge 'C' power station on 7 April 2005 finds No 66563 in charge of 6E36, the 0555 departure from Hunterston. Within minutes of its arrival, the locomotive crawls forward into the discharge shed. On the left is the discharge facility for barges on the Aire & Calder Navigation.

Each HHA wagon is divided into four compartments, each containing up to 17 tonnes of coal. At Ferrybridge trains can be discharged from either of the two tracks, but it is very rare for both tracks to be used at the same time.

The first wagons of 6E36 emerge from the discharge shed, their contents having been conveyed either to the power station stockpile or direct to one of the burners. The door-closing equipment in the foreground is used only by traditional mgr hoppers, not by the new generation of bogie wagons operated by Freightliner and EWS.

It can take as little as 45 minutes to empty a 19-wagon train, although the schedule allows a safe margin and each train is usually on site for around 1 hour 30 minutes. The next journey for this set of wagons is from Ferrybridge to Redcar, to collect another load of coal for Ferrybridge.

2.

South Wales

ew regions of Great Britain had a closer association with coal than the South Wales valleys. The dense network of lines radiating from Newport, Cardiff and Swansea was geared largely to the needs of 19th-century pit owners, who needed an efficient means of transporting their product to the South Wales ports and to domestic customers. The topography of the region, with its narrow, steep-sided valleys, gave the network its distinctive shape, with some pitheads lying only a mile or two apart as the crow flies, but separated by a mountain ridge and therefore reached by different branches of the railway. By the 1970s the network was already heavily rationalised, largely as a result of pit closures. Yet much of the remaining route mileage was still dominated by coal, with more than 60 rail-connected pits forwarding a total of around 16 million tonnes a year. The train plan was varied and complex, ranging from the slick merry-go-round operation at Aberthaw power station to export movements in unfitted mineral wagons and short-haul journeys to washeries and coking plants.

Aberthaw 'B' power station was equipped for

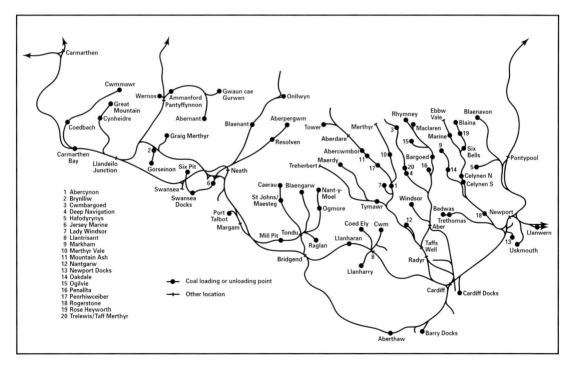

South Wales railways in the early 1970s, showing coal loading and unloading points.

Class 25 locomotives Nos 7518 and 7516, later renumbered 25168 and 25166 respectively, arrive at Castle Pond exchange sidings, near the former Abersychain & Talywain station on the Blaenavon branch, with unfitted mineral wagons on 21 May 1973. The Blaenavon branch was taken out of use in 1980 after the closure of Big Pit. *Tom Heavyside*

Scheduled mgr arrivals at Aberthaw, May 1971			
Days	Code	Arr time	From
MX	6O88	0215	Ocean & Taff Merthyr
MX	6O97	0649	Ocean & Taff Merthyr
MX	6O90	0750	Merthyr Vale
EWD	6O92	1120	Blaenant
EWD	6O97	1312	Grovesend
SX	6O92	1510	Blaenant
SX	6O88	1750	Lady Windsor
SX	6O92	1946	Blaenant
SX	6O89	2331	Blaenant

merry-go-round operation when it opened in 1971, but for more than a decade it remained the exception rather than the norm. In 1976 it consumed 2.1 million tons of coal, much of it originating in the Cardiff valleys. Most of the South Wales pitheads still employed old-fashioned loading methods; by 1977 only Taff Merthyr and Blaenant were equipped with rapid loading bunkers. While most South Wales coal trains in the 1970s were Class 37-hauled, merry-go-round trains to Aberthaw required the use of a Class 47

Passing Blaenant Colliery on 16 April 1982 is No 37236 with the 9B77 trip working from Onllwyn to Swansea Eastern Depot, conveying a mixture of MDO, MCO and HTV wagons.

locomotive with slow speed control. A separate merry-go-round discharge facility was provided at the nearby Aberthaw cement works.

The coal-fired power stations at Carmarthen Bay and Uskmouth still relied on traditional 16-ton and 21-ton wagons for their deliveries, which totalled some 850,000 tons in 1976. Neither power station was considered to be a worthwhile candidate for merry-go-round conversion; had it not been for political pressure they would both have closed in 1977. As things turned out, Carmarthen Bay received its last trainload of coal in 1983, while Uskmouth stopped taking rail-borne deliveries in 1984, after which it remained open but served by road.

Coking coal was an important source of revenue in the 1970s for BR's Cardiff division. This coal was sourced from pits mainly at the western end of the coalfield, such as Oakdale, Celynen South and Rose Heyworth. Some of the coking coal travelled out of the region to British Steel Corporation (BSC) coke ovens at Shotton and Scunthorpe, but the majority of the tonnage was for local consumption, including BSC plants at Llanwern, Port Talbot and East Moors, the Phurnacite plant at Abercwmboi, and coke ovens at Bedwas, Nantgarw, Cwm and Coed Ely. Some of the resulting coke was also moved by rail, with flows to Barry Docks for export and to Avonmouth for Imperial Smelting.

Anthracite was mined mainly at the western end of the South Wales coalfield. It was often moved in two stages: first to washeries such as those at Coedbach, Abernant, Gwaun-cae-Gurwen and Onllwyn, then to the final consumer, either in the form of high-quality domestic coal or as 'duff' used to increase the calorific value of poorer grades of power station coal. The traffic from pitheads to washeries totalled 3.2 million tonnes in 1977, but it covered only short distances and was subject to frequent variation. In the same year BR moved about 1.35 million tons of domestic coal from South Wales sources, with wagonload movements to concentration depots

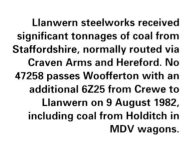

Llanwern steelworks received significant tonnages of coal from Staffordshire, normally routed via Craven Arms and Hereford. No 47258 passes Woofferton with an additional 6Z25 from Crewe to Llanwern on 9 August 1982, including coal from Holditch in MDV wagons.

RAIL FREIGHT: COAL

Class 37 No 6985, later to be renumbered 37285, passes Crumlin with a train of unfitted coke wagons for Ebbw Vale on 21 May 1973. *Tom Heavyside*

throughout the country as well as trainload movements for export.

Export traffic in the 1970s was concentrated on Swansea and Barry. The facilities at Swansea were unable to accept continuously braked rolling-stock and BR had to keep a fleet of some 10,000 unfitted mineral wagons in service just for this traffic. The discharge operation was highly labour-intensive: each wagon was uncoupled from its train and moved via a weighbridge and turntable to the hoist platform, where the wagon was tipped and its contents emptied directly into the hold of a waiting ship. Apart from the deteriorating state of the wagons, this operation was unsatisfactory because of the degradation of the coal that occurred when it fell some 30 feet into the ship.

Imported coal was still virtually unheard of in South Wales in the 1970s. A taste of things to come was the movement of 24,000 tons of Australian and American coal from Newport and Cardiff docks to Didcot power station in 1977. Further movements on this axis occurred in 1979/80; however, they ceased due to the threat of industrial action by South Wales miners.

Although by 1977 some 83% of the Cardiff division's coal traffic was moved by the trainload, most flows were far from efficient by today's standards. The rail layouts at collieries were often complex and required the use of internal shunting locomotives, including the last vestiges of steam at locations such as Mountain Ash, Brynlliw, Maesteg and Graig Merthyr. Despite the

'trainload' label, trains were often routed via one or more of the South Wales marshalling yards – Radyr, which was the focal point for all the Cardiff valleys, Llandeilo Junction, Margam and Severn Tunnel Junction. Although BR had reduced the size of the South Wales coal wagon fleet from 44,000 in the early 1970s to 32,000 in 1977, the overall wagon productivity was still poor. Moreover, coal movements placed heavy demands on management time, with some 40% of trains falling outside the mandatory train plan.

The decade of the 1980s was characterised by continuing rationalisation, both in the coal industry and on the railway. At the start of the decade almost all traffic other than that to Aberthaw was moved in unfitted or vacuum-braked wagons, and many flows were costly to operate with frequent run-round movements and shunting. The following snapshot of flows in the Tondu area in April 1982 illustrates the point:

Margam-Maesteg empties
Margam-Blaengarw empties
Maesteg-Tondu (run round)-Ogmore loaded
Blaengarw-Tondu (run round)-Ogmore loaded
Nant-y-Moel-Ogmore loaded
Ogmore-Nant-y-Moel empties
Maesteg-Margam loaded
Ogmore-Margam loaded
Maesteg-Newport Docks loaded
Ogmore-Aberthaw loaded merry-go-round

Industrial steam survived at Mountain Ash until December 1979. A Robert Stephenson & Hawthorns 'Austerity' 0-6-0ST hauls an internal train from Penrhiwceiber Colliery to Aberaman Phurnacite plant on 21 September 1979. The locomotive had been built by RSH in 1944 with works number 7139 but was rebuilt by Hunslet in 1962 as No HE3880. After finishing its industrial career it found a home on the Pontypool & Blaenavon Railway. *Tom Heavyside*

Radyr yard was the gathering point for coal from the Cardiff valleys. Class 37 No 6918 (later No 37218) waits to enter the yard with MCO wagons on 25 May 1973 while a Class 08 shunter marshals a further short rake of MCOs. No 37218 was still in use with Direct Rail Services in 2005. *Tom Heavyside*

Severn Tunnel Junction yard was the gateway marshalling point for South Wales, with trunk trains running to and from various English destinations. No 37298 heads east at Severn Tunnel Junction with a mixed coal train on 23 March 1976. The yard closed completely in 1987, with much of its work transferred to Gloucester and East Usk Junction yards. *Tom Heavyside*

In the early 1980s Tondu was a busy freight-only junction, with coal trains serving three colliery branches as well as two routes to the South Wales main line.
No 37234 sets off from Tondu on 15 April 1982 after running round its train of MDV wagons, forming 9B91 from Garw to Ogmore.

At Aberbeeg the Rose Heyworth branch diverged from the line to Ebbw Vale. No 37241 waits at Aberbeeg with the 6A85 empties for Rose Heyworth on 13 April 1982, comprising mainly MDV mineral wagons.

At Aber on 14 April 1982, Nos 37294 and 37275 take the freight-only line to Taffs Well with the 6O93 mgr service to Aberthaw power station. By using the Aber to Taffs Well line coal trains were able to avoid the busy stretch through Cardiff General (later Central) station.

After its closure to passengers in 1970, the Maesteg branch remained busy with coal to and from Maesteg Central washery, Caerau and St Johns collieries and Maesteg National Fuel Distributors depot. No 37258 shunts MDO and MDV wagons at Maesteg before departing with the 9B93 trip to Ogmore on 15 April 1982. Passenger services to Maesteg resumed in 1992.

The miners' strike of 1984/85 was a watershed that sealed the fate of many pits and, many would say, of the British coal industry as a whole. The tally of South Wales pit closures totalled eight in 1985, two in 1986, one in 1988 and five in 1989. The railway network continued to shrink as its traffic sources dried up; the branch line closures included Coed Ely in 1983, Nant-y-Moel in 1984, Rose Heyworth in 1986, Maerdy in 1986 and Cynheidre in 1989. Reduced coal traffic from the Rhymney Valley allowed BR to close the link from Aber to Taffs Well (Walnut Tree Junction) in 1982, with remaining trains diverted via Cardiff Central. The Maesteg branch would have closed in the early 1990s after the last of the coal had been removed from stocks at the closed pit; however, the track was retained for re-opening to passenger traffic.

Positive developments included the opening of Betws drift mine in the late 1970s, with underground conveyors feeding a rapid loading bunker on the site of Ammanford colliery. At Oakdale new loading facilities were provided in the early 1980s that would also handle the output from Markham and Celynen South pits, linked to Oakdale by underground roadways. In the far west of the region, BR opened its new link from Coedbach to Kidwelly in 1983 to allow closure of the Burry Port & Gwendraeth Valley line from

Although dating back to 1910, Oakdale Colliery was modernised in the late 1970s with underground links from neighbouring pits at Celynen North and Markham. No 37255 passes under the loading bunker at Oakdale on 13 April 1982 before working 6A94 to Llanwern.

The restricted loading gauge on the Burry Port & Gwendraeth Valley line forced BR to use Class 03 locomotives with cut-down cabs. Nos 03145, 03382 and 03141 approach Pembrey with loaded MDO wagons from Coedbach on 16 April 1982. The section of line between Coedbach and Pembrey closed in September 1983 when BR opened a new connection with the main line near Kidwelly.

Coedbach to Burry Port. The latter route had a severe loading gauge restriction, which required the use of Class 03 locomotives with cut-down cabs.

The use of unfitted and vacuum-braked wagons declined naturally as many of the flows that used them ceased, and air-braked stock gradually took over the remaining business. Domestic coal for national distribution was transferred to air-braked wagons in 1983/84 in readiness for the closure of BR's vacuum-braked wagonload network. Inward movements to the Phurnacite plant at Abercwmboi were also converted to air-braked operation. Even the self-contained flow of opencast coal from Cwmmawr to Coedbach became air-braked in the late 1980s, requiring the

provision of air-braked Class 08 shunters with cut-down cabs.

The anachronistic sight of unfitted wagons on export traffic to Swansea finally ceased with the introduction of containers for the Northern Irish market from late 1986. The lion's share of that traffic was conveyed in Cawoods containers from Coedbach and other loading points to Ellesmere Port, giving a much longer rail haul than previously. Smaller tonnages were moved in Kellys containers to Swansea. However, the use of vacuum-braked stock for some Swansea-bound coal, and on export traffic from Trelewis to Newport Docks, was to continue until the end of the decade.

Spoil from Taff Merthyr and Deep Navigation pits was conveyed to a tip at Penallta Junction, using HKV hopper wagons that had originally been built for iron ore traffic. No 37264 waits while its train is discharged at Penallta Junction on 13 April 1982.

Aberaman Phurnacite plant, usually known as Abercwmboi by BR, was a major source of inward and outward coal traffic until its closure in 1990. No 37225 prepares to depart with MDO and HTO wagons for Lady Windsor Colliery on 14 April 1982. On the left is No 37300 with a mixed load of domestic coal for sorting at Radyr – the destinations included Stonehouse, Bristol Wapping Wharf, Swansea Burrows, Gobowen, Newtown, Taplow, Plaistow and Chelmsford.

The British Steel Corporation switched to overseas sources for much of its coking coal, using its deep water berth at Port Talbot, and in January 1989 BR started an intensive service in merry-go-round wagons from Port Talbot Grange Sidings to Llanwern. Perhaps it was no coincidence that the extensively modernised pit at Oakdale, which produced mainly coking coal for British Steel, was announced for closure in the summer of that year. The Port Talbot to Llanwern flow became the first coal service in South Wales to use Class 56 traction regularly, breaking the long-standing near-monopoly of the Class 37s.

By January 1990 only six deep mines remained in South Wales: Tower, Taff Merthyr, Deep Navigation, Penallta, Blaenant and Betws. Further casualties halved that total within two years: geological faults were blamed for the premature closure of Blaenant in 1990, while Penallta and Deep Navigation both wound their last coal in 1991. Another loss to the South Wales coal industry was the closure of Abercwmboi Phurnacite plant in 1990, despite recent investment in merry-go-round discharge facilities at the plant.

Then came British Coal's controversial announcement in autumn 1992 that it was to close 31 of its 50 pits nationwide within six months.

The hit list included Taff Merthyr and Betws, leaving only Tower as a working reminder of the once thriving mining industry of South Wales. The closure of Taff Merthyr went ahead as planned in 1993, bringing with it the closure of Radyr yard, which had been steadily run down over a period of years. Betws was to survive for another decade after its transfer to the private sector, albeit with a relatively small output which in later years was distributed by road.

Tower was the subject of a management buyout in January 1995 and maintained a healthy output into the 21st century, outliving all other management buyouts of British mines. For a time coal from Tower was carried by road to Cwmgwrach for onward movement by rail to Aberthaw; however, late 1997 saw the resumption of merry-go-round loading at the pit. In 2005 Tower still had reserves for another five years, although there were ominous reports of geological difficulties that might well shorten its life.

While deep mining faced terminal decline, opencasting was a growth industry in South Wales, as it was in other regions. By 1996 Celtic Energy,

which had bought out the South Wales assets of British Coal Opencast, operated nine opencast sites and five rail-connected washeries and distribution points. In 1997 the company secured a contract with National Power for the supply of 3.5 million tonnes of coal to Aberthaw over a five-year period, countering fears that National Power might opt for a total switch to imported fuel.

The busiest Celtic Energy distribution point in the mid-1990s was Coedbach, which produced a wide range of rail traffic: containerised anthracite duff to Immingham for the manufacture of briquettes, containerised household coal for Ireland via Cardiff Docks, containerised coal for mainland Europe via Swansea Docks, anthracite 'sweetener' for Aberthaw power station, and household coal for several regional distribution depots.

A new loading point for Celtic Energy in 1996 was Parc Slip, located on the Bridgend to Tondu freight line near the site of the former Mill Pit colliery. The coal from Parc Slip was destined both for power stations such as Didcot and Ironbridge and for industrial users such as Blue Circle Cement at Westbury and Plymstock. In the period 2002-05 Parc Slip also dispatched trains to Hope and Rugby for the cement industry, and to Onllwyn for blending.

Meanwhile the independent company Ryan Mining had received a £4.25 million Government Section 8 grant in 1993 to build a new coal loading facility at Cwmgwrach in the Vale of Neath. The scheme involved re-opening 6 miles of the former Aberpergwm branch, which had last been used in 1985, and the loading facility would handle coal from Ryan mines at Pentreclwydau, Lyn, Venallt and Rheola. It was the first facility of its kind to have a computerised blending system capable of mixing different grades of coal to provide the calorific value specified by the end user.

Coal returned to the Garw Valley branch in 1991 when BR was contracted to move nearly 500,000 tonnes of coal from the site of three former collieries, the last of which had closed in 1985. The traffic was the result of a multi-million pound land reclamation scheme funded by the Welsh Development Agency. BR used rakes of its newly introduced MEA box wagons to move the coal to a blending site at Jersey Marine, Neath, before final delivery to Aberthaw.

Sample coal programme for Aberthaw, April 1995			
Days	Code	Arr time	From
EWD	7C01	0649	Cwmbargoed
MWFO	7C21	0820	Cardiff Docks (blending site)
SX	7C03	0947	Cwmbargoed
SO	7C03	1014	Cwmbargoed
EWD	7C04	1216	Cwmgwrach
SX	7Z16	1408	Avonmouth
SO	7Z28	1413	Cwmbargoed
SX	7Z17	1546	Avonmouth
SX	7C06	1628	Cwmgwrach
MThFSO	7C07	1903	Cwmbargoed
FSX	7C19	2103	Steel Supply, Jersey Marine
SuO	7C34	1537	Cwmbargoed
SuO	7C35	1714	Cwmbargoed
SuO	7C36	2125	Cwmbargoed

A more modest reclamation scheme saw the rail movement of coal for Onyx Land Technology from Brynteg, on the Onllwyn branch. In this instance no siding was provided but trains simply stopped on the branch for loading from a lineside pad. The traffic started in 1998 with trainloads of containers to Barry. Trains later operated from Brynteg to Cwmgwrach for blending, and to Aberthaw direct.

On the negative side, the last train of opencast coal from Cwmmawr to Coedbach ran in 1996, and the Coedbach processing facility itself closed in 1998, with most of its flows diverted to operate from Onllwyn instead. The disposal point at Gwaun-cae-Gurwen was mothballed in 1999, effectively bringing the closure of the 6-mile branch from Pantyffynnon. The output from Cwmbargoed declined in the 1990s and its only use by the end of the decade was for Tarmac roadstone traffic. The future of this remote outpost perched high above Merthyr Tydfil seemed more hopeful in 2005 when the developer Miller Argent received planning permission to

After a long history dominated by coal exports, Swansea Docks followed the national trend and switched to handling imported coal. No 66201 waits while its train is loaded with coal for Aberthaw on 20 July 2001.

move more than 10 million tonnes of coal in connection with the Ffos-y-Fran land reclamation project. However, the planning permission was later quashed.

A severe rail freight loss in 2002 was the regular and high-volume flow of imported coal from Port Talbot to Llanwern for Corus (formerly British Steel), following the end of steel-making at Llanwern and the restructuring of Corus operations in South Wales. The loading facility at Grange Sidings, Port Talbot, was too good to be abandoned and soon found itself handling coal for the power generators, albeit on a smaller scale than when it served Llanwern.

With the continued contraction of mining in South Wales, it was no surprise when National Power started using imported coal to supplement its supplies at Aberthaw. In 1995 Transrail, the BR freight division responsible for most freight operations in the west and north-west of Britain in the run-up to privatisation, was providing Aberthaw with a modest total of two daily trainloads from Avonmouth import terminal. By 2001 the power station was taking imported coal through Swansea and Port Talbot as well as Avonmouth, though still with regular traffic from South Wales sources as well. Other port terminals that supplied Aberthaw in 2004/05 were Portbury and Newport.

Sample coal programme for Aberthaw, May 2001

Days	Code	Arr time	From
TWThO	6G53	0055	Newport Docks
MX	6B72	0046	Avonmouth
MTX	6G64	0605	Newport Docks
MX	6G60	1010	Newport Docks
SO	6G42	1100	Avonmouth
SX	6B68	1123	Avonmouth
SX	6G47	1210	Avonmouth
FSO	6C31	1245	Cwmgwrach
EWD	6G44	1410	Newport Docks
SX	6C45	1600	Tower
SX	6B85	1610	Avonmouth
ThO	6G78	1715	Steel Supply, Jersey Marine
SX	6B77	1915	Avonmouth
SX	6G62	1930	Newport Docks
SX	6G49	2001	Avonmouth
MSX	6C47	2057	Tower
MSX	7O11	2315	Onllwyn

The railway system at Newport Docks was virtually disused by the mid-1990s, but was revived in 1997 for flows of steel and imported coal. The first coal flow came from the Westland Coal site in the docks, and comprised two or three weekly trainloads of MEA wagons to Rugby for final delivery by road to New Bilton cement works. In 1999 Associated British Ports provided a new loading facility and run-round loop for further flows of imported coal, with the main destination expected to be Fifoots Point.

Fifoots Point was the new name for Uskmouth 'B' power station, which had been closed by its owner, National Power, in 1995 in the light of increased competition from gas and the government directive to reduce emissions from coal-fired stations. Since the mid-1980s Uskmouth had received its coal by road and the rail terminal had been decommissioned; however,

No 66046 arrives at the then recently re-opened Uskmouth (Fifoots Point) power station with 6Z91, the 1104 from East Usk Junction, on 25 October 2000. The coal had been moved from Avonmouth the previous day.

the short branch line from East Usk Junction was left in place, albeit heavily overgrown.

The revival of the power station happened under unusual circumstances. The facility had been sold for scrap to demolition contractor Cox & Company, who then resold it in February 1998 to the multinational company AES Electric – a relatively new name in Britain but already the largest independent power generator in the world, with 137 power stations spread across several continents. Under AES ownership the name Uskmouth gave way to Fifoots Point, which is the nearest physical landmark to the power station's location.

The use of rail transport was an integral part of AES Electric's rebuilding plans for Fifoots Point right from the start. Ironically the only part of the original rail system still extant was the tippler discharge mechanism, which rotated individual wagons to empty their load on to an underground conveyor. Unfortunately this process was incompatible with modern air-braked wagons and AES Electric therefore provided an entirely new hopper discharge facility. The total cost of restoring the rail terminal was £4.2 million.

Following trials in early 2000 Fifoots Point was soon receiving regular deliveries of coal in HAA merry-go-round wagons from Parc Slip, Newport Docks and Avonmouth. EWS also won the contract to supply the flue gas desulphurisation plant at Fifoots Point with lime from Dowlow, using a small fleet of CSA wagons specially refurbished for the purpose. However, market conditions soon turned against AES Electric and in early 2002 production at Fifoots Point came to an abrupt end as the company went into receivership.

Limited production resumed at Fifoots Point to cover peak demand in the winter of 2003/04. The power station was then sold to Uskmouth Power Company, with its name changed back to Uskmouth, and coal trains started running again from Newport Docks in August 2004. However, the amount of coal delivered each week was smaller than in 2001 and there was no sign of the lime traffic restarting.

Still in obsolete Trainload Coal livery, No 37894 passes Briton Ferry with 6E12, the 1925 from Swansea Burrows to Doncaster Belmont, on 28 August 1998. The Russells containers are carrying coal from Onllwyn to Hull, having recently been displaced from the flow to Coal Products Limited at Immingham.

3.

Southern England

In the early 1970s the Kent coalfield was still producing rail traffic from three locations: Tilmanstone, Snowdown and Betteshanger. Both Tilmanstone and Snowdown were reached from the Faversham to Dover line and served by pick-up goods trains, including shunter-operated trips on the short branch to Tilmanstone from Shepherds Well. The service from Betteshanger was mainly trainload and included up to four daily departures for the London Midland Region together with one service to Southfleet.

By the early 1980s only Betteshanger remained, which continued to produce coal for the steel and cement industries, with booked departures to Toton yard and Halling cement works. BR managed to enhance productivity by combining the northbound flow from Betteshanger to Toton with southbound coal from the Midlands to Ridham Dock; the wagons ran empty from Ridham Dock to Betteshanger for reloading. However, the days of the Kent coalfield were already numbered and Betteshanger closed in 1989.

The cement and paper industries in Kent generated several trainload coal flows. One of the longest-running flows of its kind was to the APCM (later Blue Circle) cement works at Northfleet. The terminal at Northfleet was adapted for merry-go-round operation in the early 1970s and continued to receive coal trains from Yorkshire via Toton yard until the early 1990s. The sources of the coal in later years included Grimethorpe and South Kirkby collieries. A separate coal receiving terminal at Southfleet, reached by a branch from the Bromley to Maidstone line, had closed in 1976.

The Rugby Cement works at Halling received coal by rail until the 1980s, with merry-go-round services operating from Betteshanger. A surprising twist occurred in 1989 when BR moved coal out of Halling, destined for Foxton.

A number of freight yards on the Southern Region had catenary installed to allow Class 71 electrics to operate in overhead mode. No 71008 waits to depart from Snowdown colliery with loaded MCV mineral wagons for Workington on 17 September 1974. *Tom Heavyside*

Right The Kent coalfield produced good coking coal that was consumed by various steel plants in northern England. 'Peak' No 45061 heads north on the Midland main line near Souldrop with loaded HTV hoppers on 1 July 1981.

Right In turn, the paper and cement industries in North Kent received much of their coal from the Midlands and northern England. Electro-diesels Nos 73133 and 73121 head an mgr working for Ridham Dock through Rochester on 10 June 1981.

Below Shortly before the final stage of the Leicester re-signalling scheme was commissioned, No 56102 passes Finedon Road sidings, Wellingborough, with 7O85, the 1323 Toton to Northfleet mgr train, on 14 August 1987. The sidings contain a large number of HTV hopper wagons awaiting their fate.

The Bowaters (later UK Paper) paper mill at Sittingbourne received coal by rail for many years, using the company's merry-go-round discharge terminal at Ridham Dock. Among the regular points of origin were Butterwell in Northumberland and Oxcroft in Derbyshire. The Reeds paper mill at Brookgate, on the Hoo Junction to Maidstone line, was equipped with merry-go-round discharge facilities in 1986 and also received trains from Oxcroft. For a short period in the early 1990s both paper companies switched to using imported coal, which was moved by rail from Thamesport; however, the sourcing reverted to the Midlands before the traffic ceased altogether. The import terminal at Thamesport later handled short-term coal flows to Ipswich and Norwich for the sugar refining industry, and to Slough for Slough Estates.

To the north of London, the cement industry sponsored trainload coal services to Foxton, Tring and Chinnor, as well as wagonload deliveries to Claydon near Ipswich. The Rugby Cement works at Foxton (properly known as Barrington) switched to using imported coal and was receiving

In the early 1990s BR carried imported coal from Grain (Thamesport) to Brookgate and Ridham Dock for the paper industry. Despite being allocated to Trainload Construction, No 56001 *Whatley* heads along the Grain branch with 6Z60, the 0950 Hoo Junction to Grain empty mgr train, on 23 December 1992.

regular merry-go-round deliveries from King's Lynn in the late 1980s. That traffic ceased in 1993 when King's Lynn Docks closed to rail traffic, but deliveries of coal to Foxton restarted from Immingham in 1995 and were still taking place in 2005, including some trial movements by Freightliner Heavy Haul. Other ports that supplied Foxton after 1995 were Hull, Avonmouth and Newport.

Tring Cutting cement works continued to receive coal by rail until 1990. In later years the coal was supplied from Coventry colliery, which produced the unusual sight of an electrically hauled merry-go-round train on the West Coast Main Line. Chinnor cement works stopped taking rail-borne deliveries in 1989 because the vacuum-braked wagons used on the flow were life-expired and there was no prospect of investment in new wagons and discharge facilities. Chinnor had received both home-produced coal from Clipstone and imported coal from King's Lynn in its later years. Claydon cement works was served by BR's wagonload coal network until the withdrawal of the East Anglian Speedlink Coal service in the early 1990s.

In the west of England, the cement industry generated coal traffic in trainload volumes at several locations. The Blue Circle works at Westbury was served by BR's wagonload coal network from the late 1980s but reverted to trainload operation in the 1990s, with trains

Right Chinnor cement works continued to receive deliveries of coal in HTV hoppers until December 1989. Nos 20186 and 20105 leave Chinnor with empty hoppers for Toton on 20 August 1986. The train will run round at Princes Risborough and wait for a path between passenger services on the single line to Banbury.

Below Coal for Tring Cutting (Pitstone) cement works brought the otherwise unusual sight of a Class 58-hauled mgr train to the southern stretch of the West Coast Main Line. No 58017 approaches Leighton Buzzard with 7R19, the 1013 from Three Spires Junction to Tring, on 1 August 1990.

running mainly from Parc Slip. A shorter-lived flow of coal operated from Parc Slip to Plymstock cement works from 1997 until 1999, using MEA wagons as far as Tavistock Junction yard with final delivery to the works by road. At Avonmouth, the Commonwealth Smelting works received trainloads of coke from Port Talbot in vacuum-braked hopper wagons until the late 1980s.

●

While the CEGB concentrated its 1960s power station building programme largely on coal-producing regions, an important exception was Didcot, some 75 miles from the nearest colliery. Production at the 2,000MW Didcot station began in 1972 and BR soon built up an intensive merry-go-round schedule from pits across the Midlands. In the 1970s and early 1980s Didcot also took short-term deliveries of imported coal from Newport and Cardiff, and Welsh coal from Mill

Left The Blue Circle cement works at Westbury was equipped for mgr operation and received deliveries in HDA hopper wagons. No 08935 approaches Westbury station with 21 empty HDAs from the cement works on 29 July 1987. They will be attached to 6A05, the 1039 Speedlink Coal service to Didcot. After the demise of Speedlink Coal, Westbury switched to receiving trainloads of coal from Toton.

Below left One of the dedicated South Wales Metals Class 37/9 locomotives, No 37906, departs from the Commonwealth Smelting sidings at Avonmouth on 31 July 1987 with 6B22, the 0939 coke empties to Margam Abbey. The locomotive had just brought in the loaded HTVs on the right.

Right Of all the new coal-fired power stations commissioned in the late 1960s and early 1970s, Didcot was the furthest away from coal mining areas. BR moved huge volumes of coal from Midlands collieries to Didcot until the shift to imported coal took place in the early 1990s. No 58040 *Cottam Power Station* departs from Didcot with 6M06, the 1915 mgr empties to Coalville Mantle Lane, on 31 July 1987.

Pit and Llanharan. However, rail carryings to Didcot slumped after the 1984/85 miners' strike as road hauliers took advantage of a relaxation in planning constraints that had been granted by the local council during the strike.

A major change came in the 1990s as Didcot's new owner, National Power, switched to using imported coal, conveyed by rail from Avonmouth. Once the Avonmouth flow was established, deliveries from other sources such as Daw Mill and the remnants of the Nottinghamshire coalfield tended to operate only on a short-term basis. The rail access to Didcot power station had been designed with west-facing access to cater for traffic from the Midlands, forcing the first trains from

Avonmouth to travel to Reading and back in order to run round; however, the track layout at Didcot was later altered to allow run-round movements just outside Didcot station.

National Power decided against installing flue gas desulphurisation equipment at Didcot. Instead, three of the four generating units were converted for dual firing with gas or coal, a change that would result in some loss of rail traffic. In 2005 it was announced that the power station would fulfil part of its renewable energy obligation by replacing 5% of its coal consumption with biomass, again leading to a potential reduction in rail traffic.

The plans for a new coal import terminal

No 66201 is pictured at Avonmouth Bulk Terminal on 28 July 2004 while its train is loaded with coal for Didcot. At that time the terminal was also producing traffic for Rugeley and Aberthaw.

Scheduled coal trains to Didcot, May 1983

Days	Code	Arr time	From
MX	7V95	0030	Bescot
MX	7V51	0125	Barrow Hill
MX	7V20	0305	Bagworth
MX	7V03	0415	Coalville Mantle Lane
MX	7V12	0530	Toton
MX	7V22	0645	Barrow Hill
MX	7V34	0830	Toton
MX	7V04	0935	Toton
SX	7V46	1045	Toton
SX	7V44	1145	Three Spires Junction
SX	7V57	1350	Barrow Hill
SX	7V63	1450	Three Spires Junction
SX	7V65	1650	Bagworth
SX	7V85	1745	Toton
SX	7V07	1900	Barrow Hill
SX	7V02	1950	Coalfields Farm
SX	7V90	2225	Three Spires Junction
SX	7V19	2315	Barrow Hill

NB Not all the above trains would run on any given day.

Sample coal programme for Didcot, February 1997

Days	Code	Arr time	From
MSX	6C70	0500	Avonmouth
SX	6C62	0635	Avonmouth
SO	6C63	0814	Avonmouth
SX	6C64	1408	Avonmouth
SX	6C65	1525	Avonmouth
MThX	7B35	1710	Parc Slip

serving Didcot go back to the late 1980s, when the preferred location was the deep-water port of Milford Haven. However, by 1991 the railway and electricity supply industries had agreed on a new site at Avonmouth, reducing the length of the rail haul to Didcot by more than half.

At Avonmouth, designers from BR's Trainload Coal division worked together with newly formed generating company National Power and the Bristol Port Company to create a facility capable of loading up to 5 million tonnes of coal a year imported through Royal Portbury Dock, on the opposite side of the Avon estuary. The coal would arrive at Portbury on 120,000-tonne ships and pass underneath the Avon estuary to the rail terminal on a specially built conveyor. The rail terminal was equipped with two overhead 2,500-tonne silos

for the rapid loading of merry-go-round trains. The project also included upgrading the freight-only line from Avonmouth to Filton and providing two 3½-mile running loops on the busy stretch between Swindon and Didcot.

The first revenue-earning services out of Avonmouth ran in August 1993. The build-up of traffic was slower than anticipated, but the flow to Didcot operated for most of the period between

1994 and 2005, and there was intermittent traffic to other power stations including Aberthaw, Rugeley, Ironbridge and Fifoots Point. In 2002 Avonmouth became one of the first locations to load coal into EWS's new bogie HTA wagons. One immediate benefit of that change was that the empties from Didcot to Avonmouth could run Class 4, ie at 75mph, on the Great Western main line.

A second coal loading terminal at Avonmouth was opened by the firm Bennetts. Most of the traffic from Bennetts was for industrial use, and the destinations included Rugby, Foxton, Plymouth and Doncaster. However, Bennetts also dispatched some coal to Aberthaw in 2004.

Royal Portbury Dock gained its own rail connection in 2001 when Railtrack re-opened 6 miles of the former Portishead branch and provided new sidings for loading coal and general freight. The scheme benefited from a £15.6 million Freight Facilities Grant, the largest such

grant that had ever been awarded. The Portishead branch had last seen revenue-earning freight traffic in 1981, although it had also been used by special trains commemorating the 150th anniversary of the Great Western Railway in 1985. The branch was relaid as single-track, but with a passing loop at the Bristol end to provide increased capacity.

The first loaded coal train left Portbury on 7 January 2002. The main destinations in the early days were Ironbridge and Fifoots Point, although the latter flow was short-lived because of the customer's demise. In 2004/05 trains ran from Portbury to Rugeley, Rugby and Foxton, although the overall traffic volume on the new line was disappointing.

Didcot power station switched to using mainly imported coal in the mid-1990s. No 60017 arrives at the power station on 27 July 2000 with 6A65, the 0851 departure from Avonmouth. It will run round here in order to enter the power station loop.

4.

The West Midlands and Staffordshire

Although coal was never the dominant industry in the West Midlands, there were significant pockets of mining in both Warwickshire and Staffordshire. Many of the smaller pits had become worked out in the middle of the 20th century, but the BR network in the late 1970s still served five pits in Warwickshire, three in South Staffordshire and six in North Staffordshire. By 2000 only one of those pits, Daw Mill in Warwickshire, remained.

At the southern end of the Warwickshire coalfield was Coventry colliery, also known as Keresley, which lay at the end of a 2-mile branch from Three Spires Junction, on the Coventry to Nuneaton line. In the 1980s the colliery dispatched merry-go-round trains to several destinations including Didcot power station, Garston Docks for export to Ireland, and Tring cement works. Alongside the colliery was Keresley Homefire coking plant, which in later years received trainloads of coal from Nottinghamshire and dispatched wagonloads of smokeless fuel for national distribution.

Coventry colliery closed in November 1991, just before the British Coal review that would threaten more than half of the nation's remaining deep mines with closure. Given that Coventry still had worthwhile reserves, the private company Coal Investments took a 15-year lease on the site and restarted production in March 1995, having also restored the rail access from Three Spires Junction. Unfortunately, however, the expense

On 18 June 1973 Class 25 No 5175 (later renumbered 25025) passes the site of Brownhills station with 8M01 from Treeton to Spring Vale, conveying coke for the iron and steel industry in the Black Country. The unfitted coke hoppers, later coded HCO, were nearing the end of their lives.
Michael Mensing

THE WEST MIDLANDS AND STAFFORDSHIRE

Above No 24091 enters Stoke-on-Trent station with a down train of unfitted 21-ton mineral wagons on 10 June 1977. The placing of a brake-van at each end of the train helped to make run-round movements easier. *Tom Heavyside*

Below No 58022 departs from the Coventry colliery exchange sidings at Three Spires Junction with 7Z60, the 1330 mgr train to Didcot, on 19 August 1985. At that time there was also inward coal traffic to Keresley Homefire plant, adjacent to Coventry colliery.

Above Daw Mill colliery kept the coal mining industry alive in the West Midlands in the 21st century, with continued investment enabling it to increase its output. As well as producing steam coal for power stations, the colliery supplied fuel for the domestic and Irish markets. No 56134 is about to depart with the 1330 Cawoods container train to Seaforth on 28 October 1993.

Below In the 1990s Washwood Heath yard remained busy as a staging point for coal trains in the West Midlands, especially workings to and from Daw Mill colliery. No 58016 has just arrived in the yard with 7A23, the 1804 from Daw Mill to Ratcliffe, on 10 June 1998.

was wasted, as the company went into receivership in 1996 before any trains had run.

The third and final chapter in the story of Coventry colliery was the redevelopment of the site as Prologis distribution park. Rail access was restored to the site as a planning requirement, but by late 2005 no customer had yet signed up to using it – a sad state of affairs and by no means unique.

A second colliery in the Coventry area that remained active in the 1970s was Newdigate, reached by a branch from the Nuneaton line just south of Bedworth; Newdigate closed in 1982.

Daw Mill colliery was UK Coal's most productive mine in the first years of the 21st century, achieving an output of 2.2 million tonnes in 2003 and 3.0 million tonnes in 2004. Originally Daw Mill was nothing more than a ventilation shaft for the nearby Dexter colliery, but became a colliery in its own right in 1965 when the shaft was modified for coal winding. Its future in 2005 seemed relatively bright, with nearly 40 million tonnes of reserves contained in the group of seams forming the Warwickshire Thick. UK Coal announced plans to invest £20 million in new coal cutting and other equipment at the colliery.

In the 1980s and 1990s Daw Mill produced coal for power generation, for industry and for domestic use; it also acted as a blending site for coal mined elsewhere. The main destinations for power station coal were Rugeley 'B' and Ironbridge, but services also operated when required to the Trent Valley power stations and to Didcot. In BR days the flows to Rugeley and Ironbridge were closely intertwined, but in 1994-96 they were operated by different companies – Mainline Freight to Rugeley and Transrail to Ironbridge. In 2005 the main destinations served from Daw Mill were Rugeley and Ratcliffe; regular services were operated by EWS, but trials were also carried out by Freightliner Heavy Haul.

Other trainload services operating out of Daw Mill included seasonal trainloads of industrial coal to Bicester for the Ministry of Defence and occasional trainloads of domestic coal for export to Northern Ireland in Cawoods containers. The Cawoods train was still in the timetable in 2004, although sightings of the distinctive yellow containers were becoming fewer and further

Scheduled mgr trains to Ironbridge and Rugeley 'B', May 1975	
Days	**Train details**
MX	6G38 0406 Stafford-Ironbridge
SX	6G38 0700 Silverdale-Ironbridge
SO	6G42 0713 Norton-Ironbridge
SX	6G42 0910 Norton-Ironbridge
SX	6G38 1116 Silverdale-Ironbridge
SX	6G38 1608 Silverdale-Ironbridge
SX	6G36 1751 Hem Heath-Ironbridge
SX	6G46 0519 Hem Heath-Rugeley
SO	6G46 0635 Hem Heath-Rugeley
EWD	6G45 0630 Coalville Mantle Lane-Rugeley
SX	6G46 0853 Hem Heath-Rugeley
SO	6G46 1030 Hem Heath-Rugeley
SX	6G37 1020 Kidsgrove-Rugeley
SX	6G46 1245 Hem Heath-Rugeley
SX	6G45 1412 Coalville Mantle Lane-Rugeley
SX	6G46 1732 Hem Heath-Rugeley
SX	6G46 1835 Hem Heath-Rugeley

between. Some domestic coal for British consumption was also railed from Daw Mill, using Network Coal services until they were abandoned, then in occasional block loads.

Birch Coppice and Baddesley collieries were closed in 1986 and 1989 respectively. They were both reached by a freight-only branch from Kingsbury, on the Birmingham to Tamworth line. The spur to Baddesley was abandoned but the branch from Kingsbury to Birch Coppice was re-opened in 2002 for movements of Volkswagen car parts from mainland Europe via the Channel Tunnel, a flow that was still operating in 2005.

Coal-mining in South Staffordshire in the 1970s was centred on three pits, West Cannock, Lea Hall and Littleton; the first to close was West Cannock, while the others survived until 1990 and 1993 respectively.

Lea Hall colliery was situated alongside the Rugeley power station complex and sent most of its output by conveyor to Rugeley 'A' station. Lea

Leaving West Cannock exchange sidings on 4 March 1975 with a brake-van in tow is No 25079, having just arrived with a rake of unfitted mineral wagons. After the closure of West Cannock colliery BR continued to carry coal from two nearby opencast railheads at Mid Cannock and Essington. *Michael Mensing*

Coal for Rugeley 'A' power station was conveyed in vacuum-braked wagons to the adjacent Lea Hall colliery. Nos 20073 and 20099 pass Hednesford with the 7T58 trip working from Mid Cannock opencast site to Lea Hall on 16 April 1986.

Hall was also the receiving point for coal supplied to Rugeley 'A' from other pits such as Holditch and Coalfields Farm; that traffic was still carried in vacuum-braked HTV wagons as late as 1988. The only outward traffic from Lea Hall was domestic coal, latterly using HEA wagons and tripped to Bescot yard as required.

Littleton colliery was reached by a 3½-mile branch from the Wolverhampton to Stafford line, with exchange sidings located just south of Penkridge station. In later years Littleton dispatched merry-go-round trains to Rugeley 'B', Ironbridge and Didcot power stations, as well as some wagonload movements of domestic coal. Each Didcot train was usually tripped to Bescot in two portions because the track layout at the exchange sidings restricted the train length for southbound departures.

Opencast mining in the Cannock area produced a significant volume of rail traffic, with loading points at Essington Wood and Mid Cannock on the Walsall to Rugeley line. The Essington Wood site was commissioned in 1982 and had a relatively short existence, while Mid Cannock was active until the mid-1980s and was used again as a disposal point for Bleak House from 1994 until 1999.

●

The North Staffordshire coalfield once covered an area of more than 70 square miles, with pits scattered in and around the industrial district of the Potteries. After the closure in 1977 of Norton pit, reached by a spur from the freight-only branch to Leek Brook Junction and Caldon Low, those North Staffordshire pits still producing rail traffic were Wolstanton, Hem Heath (also known as Trentham), Holditch and Silverdale.

Wolstanton and Hem Heath both lay on the main north-south railway route through the Potteries. Wolstanton closed in 1986, while Hem Heath was abandoned in 1996, having been run by Coal Investments after its closure by British Coal in 1992. Although coal had been mined at Hem Heath since the 1920s, the pit was substantially rebuilt in 1950 with a new shaft that was to be the third deepest in the country. In later years coal from nearby Florence pit was also brought to the surface at Hem Heath. Rail services operated from Hem Heath to several major power stations including Ironbridge and Rugeley 'B', as well as to ICI at Northwich and the British Steel Corporation at Llanwern.

Holditch and Silverdale were reached by a freight-only branch that was formerly part of the through route from Market Drayton to Stoke-on-Trent. Access to the pits after the closure of that route was provided by a connection from the West Coast Main Line at Madeley. In later years the destinations served by rail from Holditch included Llanwern for the British Steel Corporation and Lea Hall for Rugeley 'A' power station. Holditch closed in 1989.

Silverdale pit had origins stretching back to 1830 but the National Coal Board completed a new mine on the site in 1950, which was to become the last surviving deep pit in Staffordshire, finally bowing out in December 1998. Its last operator was the independent firm Midlands Mining, who took over from bankrupt Coal Investments in 1996. Merry-go-round trains ran from Silverdale to various power stations including Ironbridge and Fiddlers Ferry.

A short-lived opencast disposal point north of Stoke-on-Trent was Chatterley Valley, dispatching coal to power stations such as Ironbridge, Rugeley 'B' and Willington from 1988 until the mid-1990s.

●

Silverdale was the last deep mine in Staffordshire, run in later years by Coal Investments, then by Midlands Mining until its closure in 1998. No 60047 draws forward at Silverdale with the 1030 mgr service to Fiddlers Ferry on 19 June 1993. On the far right is the surviving building of Silverdale station, which had closed to passengers in 1964.

Above Chatterley Valley was a short-lived opencast terminal on the north side of Stoke-on-Trent. No 58019 is pictured at the terminal on 19 June 1993, ready to work the 1302 departure to Ironbridge.

Below The opening of Ironbridge power station gave a new lease of life to the meandering branch from Madeley Junction on the Wolverhampton to Shrewsbury line. No 47196 crosses the River Severn at Ironbridge with an empty mgr train on 10 August 1982. At that time Ironbridge was scheduled to receive three trains a day from Silverdale, two from Barrow Hill and one from Trentham.

THE WEST MIDLANDS AND STAFFORDSHIRE

From the 1970s onwards Ironbridge 'B' and Rugeley 'B' power stations were the principal destinations for rail-borne coal in the West Midlands. The 1,000MW station at Ironbridge was commissioned in 1970, bringing a new lease of life to the freight-only branch from Madeley Junction on the Wolverhampton to Shrewsbury line. When the generating industry was privatised Ironbridge was allocated to National Power; it was later sold to Eastern Group (later known as TXU Europe), then to PowerGen. Ironbridge was rumoured to be facing closure in 2003 in the light of falling demand for electricity; however, it was still going strong in 2005.

In the 1980s Ironbridge took its coal from various pits in the Midlands, but by the early 1990s BR was also starting to deliver coal from Scotland, and in the early 2000s the sources of supply included import terminals at Avonmouth, Portbury, Liverpool and Hunterston, opencast railheads at Killoch, Knockshinnoch and Chalmerston, and deep mines at Daw Mill, Welbeck and Thoresby. The access to Ironbridge from the north was made easier in 1983 when BR opened the Oxley chord linking the Stafford to Wolverhampton and Wolverhampton to Shrewsbury lines.

The 1,000MW-capacity Rugeley 'B' power station was commissioned in 1972. Under privatisation it was owned first by National Power, then by Eastern Group before its sale in 2001 to International Power. In December 2005 International Power announced its decision to fit flue gas desulphurisation equipment to Rugeley

'B', enabling it to comply with the European Large Combustion Plant Directive and continue generating at full capacity beyond January 2008.

Like Ironbridge, Rugeley 'B' looked mainly to Midlands pits for its fuel in the 1970s and 1980s. An unusual source in the early 1990s, however, was Maryport opencast disposal point in Cumbria. By 2002 Rugeley was taking coal from a similar range of sources to Ironbridge, with a mixture of deep-mined, opencast and imported coal. However, one important difference was the involvement of Freightliner Heavy Haul at Rugeley, operating flows from Hunterston, Immingham and Hull.

Older power stations in the West Midlands that used to receive coal by rail included Hams Hall, Nechells (Washwood Heath), Ocker Hill (Wednesbury) and Stourport. By the mid-1980s deliveries of coal to these stations had ceased, although the Hams Hall terminal remained in use for several years receiving trainloads of fly ash from Drakelow. The site of Hams Hall was later transformed into one of the freight villages designed to attract rail-borne traffic via the Channel Tunnel.

Coal for the cement industry was handled at two locations in the Rugby district, New Bilton and Southam. Both locations were owned by Rugby Cement and both were served by a freight-only branch from Rugby, formerly part of a through route to Leamington Spa. The connection to Southam closed in August 1985 after the end of coal deliveries in vacuum-braked wagons, while the much shorter link to New

Coal trains from Scotland started to appear in the West Midlands in the early 1990s as the power generators could no longer rely on local sources of coal. No 60071 passes Sutton Park with 6E91, the 1450 Ironbridge to York empties, on 24 July 1992. The hooded HBA wagons would be forwarded to Millerhill yard for reloading at one of the Scottish opencast disposal points.

Bilton remained in use for several more years, albeit for a different customer, Redland Rooftiles. In 1997 New Bilton works started receiving its coal by rail again, using EWS's newish fleet of MEA wagons. However, the connection to the cement works was not restored; instead the coal was offloaded in Rugby Up Yard for final delivery to the works by road. In 2004/05 the usual sources of supply were Parc Slip, Avonmouth and Immingham.

Sample coal programme for the West Midlands, April 1995

Days	Train details	Company
WO	7T72 0900 Hem Heath-Ironbridge	Transrail
SX	7T73 1135 Calverton-Ironbridge	Transrail
TSO	7G19 0915 Hem Heath-Rugeley	Mainline
TSX	7G19 0645 Silverdale-Rugeley	Mainline
FSX	7G20 1130 Mid Cannock-Rugeley	Mainline
FSX	7G21 1345 Mid Cannock-Rugeley	Mainline
TWO	7V95 1700 Mid Cannock-Didcot	Mainline
EWD	7V44 0901 Daw Mill-Didcot	Mainline
SX	7V90 1922 Daw Mill-Didcot	Mainline
ThO	7V95 2041 Daw Mill-Didcot	Mainline
SX	7V30 1810 Silverdale-Didcot	Mainline
MO	7V95 1540 Silverdale-Didcot	Mainline
SuO	7Z90 1922 Daw Mill-Didcot	Mainline
SuO	7V02 1555 Daw Mill-Didcot	Mainline
SO	7P70 0500 Daw Mill-Oakleigh	Mainline
MWFO	7P67 1150 Hem Heath-Oakleigh	Mainline
ThO	7Z67 1110 Hem Heath-Llanwern	Transrail

A section of the former Rugby to Leamington Spa line remained open into the 1980s for coal traffic to Southam cement works. No 25175 has just run round its rake of empty MCV wagons at Marton Junction on 9 April 1984, ready to return along the branch to Rugby.

5.

The East Midlands

In the early 1970s the counties of Nottinghamshire, Derbyshire and Leicestershire boasted a total of more than 50 rail-connected collieries. The area bounded by Worksop, Newark, Nottingham and Chesterfield was a maze of freight-only lines, many of which had never carried a regular passenger service. In pre-nationalisation days some pits had enjoyed separate rail connections for competing companies; even in the 1970s Mansfield, Rufford and Clipstone collieries retained both ex-Midland Railway (or ex-LMS) and ex-Great Central outlets.

The Central Electricity Generating Board had chosen in the 1960s to site a string of new coal-fired power stations in the Trent Valley, close to

Midland Railway lower-quadrant signals were still in use at Rufford Colliery Junction on 14 April 1977, when Nos 20134 and 20136 were photographed heading a coal train from Clipstone. The former Midland Railway line from Mansfield South Junction to Rufford closed in 1983 and all trains from Rufford and Clipstone were diverted via the ex-Great Central route. *Dr L. A. Nixon*

51

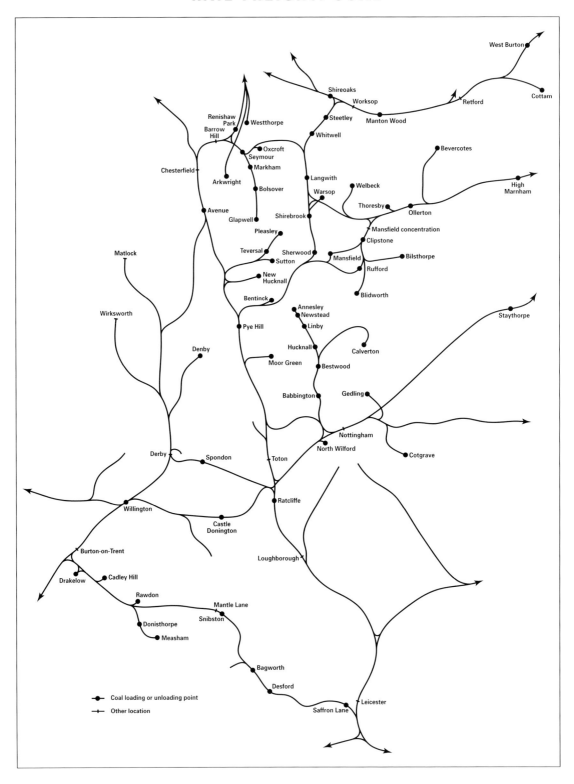

East Midlands railways in the late 1970s, showing coal loading and unloading points.

No 56085 passes Whitwell with the 6F61 empty mgr working from Cottam on 15 April 1983. On the right Nos 20008 and 20026 wait to enter Whitwell colliery sidings to collect a few wagonloads of domestic coal. Whitwell colliery closed in 1986.

copious supplies of coal and water and strategically located in the centre of the country. The first of the new power stations, West Burton, started receiving coal in 1965 ahead of its full commissioning two years later. It was at that time the largest power station in Europe and the first to be equipped for British Rail's revolutionary merry-go-round coal discharge system. By 1967 West Burton was receiving more than 1,000 trains a year, each with a payload of more than 1,000 tonnes.

By the end of the 1970s merry-go-round trains were delivering coal not only to the new Trent Valley power stations at West Burton, Cottam, Ratcliffe and Rugeley, but also to older power stations at High Marnham, Staythorpe, Castle Donington, Willington and Drakelow 'C', where the discharge facilities had been suitably adapted. The economies achieved by switching to merry-go-round operation were impressive, as a set of wagons could now be turned around in an hour instead of a day or perhaps longer. Moreover, to make the operation even more efficient BR strove to increase train lengths within the constraints of track layouts at local pits; for example, the

standard length adopted for Ratcliffe was 42 wagons, carrying a payload of up to 1,365 tonnes.

While merry-go-round traffic blossomed, coal flows in conventional vacuum-braked and unfitted wagons slowly declined. The advent of natural gas had deprived the railway of large amounts of coal traffic to gas works, and the ongoing closure of station goods yards was taking its toll on domestic coal movements. But old-style operations could still be seen in parts of the East Midlands throughout the 1970s. The power stations at Spondon, Nottingham (North Wilford) and Leicester (Saffron Lane) were never converted to merry-go-round operation, and Corby steelworks took large tonnages of East Midlands coal in conventional wagons until its closure in 1979.

The Leicestershire and Derbyshire coalfields were already in decline in the 1970s, but in

Nottinghamshire coal remained the lifeblood of many towns and districts, especially around Mansfield. Most of the larger mines in Nottinghamshire had been sunk after 1900, tapping deep seams that were expensive to reach but highly productive once the investment had been made. Among the newest pits were Calverton, sunk in 1952 and Britain's first new mine after the Second World War, Bevercotes, which opened in 1961, and Cotgrave, which opened in 1964. Miners were moving into the area to take up new jobs, many of them from North East England and the Central Belt of Scotland where mining was in sharp decline.

In Leicestershire, the emphasis shifted from deep-mined to opencast coal as underground reserves became worked out or uneconomic. New rail-served opencast disposal points opened during the 1970s at Coalfields Farm, Bagworth and Swains Park, keeping the freight-only Coalville line busy with a mixture of merry-go-round, vacuum-braked and unfitted coal trains. In those days even opencast loading points were usually equipped with overhead bunkers, giving them a permanent appearance even though in reality some were short-lived.

The shift to trainload movements in the region lessened the need for marshalling yards. The former Great Central yard at Annesley had already closed in the 1960s when BR cut out duplicate routes in the Leen Valley, while the former Great Northern marshalling yard at Colwick closed in 1970 after a long period of decline. Traffic at Mansfield Concentration Sidings, on former Great Central metals east of Mansfield, gradually died away and its role was eventually taken over by Worksop.

Even the former Midland Railway yard complex at Toton, which had acted as a gathering point for the Nottinghamshire and Derbyshire coalfields since the middle of the 19th century, began to shrink in the 1970s as more trains ran direct from pithead to power station. Hump shunting ceased in Toton down yard in 1978; all traffic requiring hump shunting was then transferred to the up yard, until that too closed in 1984. The remaining sidings at Toton were increasingly used not to shunt individual wagons but for the staging, re-manning and re-engining of merry-go-round trains.

The 1970s also saw changes on the traction front. The most significant change was the arrival of the first Class 56 locomotives in 1976 – the first BR main-line diesels built solely for heavy freight traffic and the first to be equipped for air-braked operation only. The first Class 56s were allocated to Tinsley and Toton depots and replaced older traction such as Class 47s and pairs of Class 20s on merry-go-round and other block coal workings. Further change would come in the 1980s as the Class 58s – designed essentially as a cheaper version of the Class 56 – took hold on many East Midlands coal flows.

●

'Peak' No 45064 threads its way out of Toton East Yard with 8V26, the 1551 departure to Acton, on 3 June 1981. The wagons are bound for Luton Limbury Road, Neasden and other coal concentration depots in the London area. Toton East Yard was abandoned after the 1984/85 miners' strike.

During the 1980s merry-go-round traffic became still more dominant as BR sought to increase productivity and drive down costs. The long-term contract between the NCB and the CEGB survived a probe by the Monopolies and Mergers Commission, and BR continued to provide an intensive service from local pits to the various Trent Valley power stations. Old-fashioned operations were weeded out as the opportunity arose; a case in point was the flow of coal in unfitted HUO wagons to Spondon power station, which finally ceased in 1984.

The trickle of rail-served pit closures in the early 1980s included Desford, Snibston and Measham in Leicestershire, and Babbington and Newstead in Nottinghamshire. Rail traffic from Arkwright colliery, reached by a fragment of the former Great Central main line near Staveley, ceased when the pit was linked underground to Markham. Around Mansfield the mining industry was still thriving; the only significant railway closure in that area was the former Midland Railway access to Rufford and Clipstone collieries, with traffic diverted on to the ex-Great Central route.

Then came the year-long miners' strike of 1984/85. Coal flows from Leicestershire and Derbyshire dried up quickly. However, large numbers of Nottinghamshire miners continued working throughout the strike, defying the opposition of miners from other regions who came in their thousands to picket Nottinghamshire pits. Trains therefore continued to run on certain routes, such as to Ratcliffe and High Marnham power stations.

After the strike ended in March 1985 the pace of colliery closures quickened. Between 1985 and 1989 the NCB closed a total of 13 deep mines across Leicestershire, Derbyshire and Nottinghamshire, and many more faced an uncertain future. Some compensation for the railway was provided by new opencast sites, such as Lounge on the Coalville line and Bennerley on the Erewash Valley line near Toton. But some coal consumers were already looking overseas for their future coal supplies.

The retreat of the coal industry was mirrored by economies in BR yards and locomotive depots. Among the closures of the 1980s were Bestwood Park yard, on the Leen Valley line north of Nottingham, and Westhouses locomotive depot on the Erewash Valley line. The famous

The freight-only Newstead branch served five collieries in the early 1980s. No 47364 arrives at Newstead colliery with merry-go-round empties on 14 April 1983. Although most of the rail-borne output from Newstead went in mgr trainloads, a few vacuum-braked mineral and hopper wagons can be seen in the sidings on the left. The pits in the area were all closed by 1999 and the railway became a passenger-only route for the new Nottingham-Mansfield service, later extended to Worksop.

Ratcliffe was the largest of the Trent Valley power stations, taking coal from a wide range of sources across the East Midlands. No 58004 pulls away from the power station with empties for Toton yard on 24 April 1984.

Sample coal programme for West Burton, September 1994			
Days	**Code**	**Arr time**	**From**
TWThO	7G30	0030	Harworth
TWThO	7G31	0130	Thoresby
MO	7G32	0230	Bilsthorpe
TThO	7G32	0230	Worksop (Silverdale traffic)
WO	7G32	0230	Worksop (Clipstone traffic)
FSX	7G33	0430	Harworth
MTWO	7G34	0730	Thoresby
ThO	7G34	0830	Bilsthorpe
SO	7G34	1030	Harworth
SX	7G35	1030	Kiveton Park
SO	7G35	1130	Bilsthorpe
MTWO	7G36	1130	Thoresby
MTWSO	7G37	1230	Clipstone
ThFO	7G37	1230	Kiveton Park
MTWO	7G38	1530	Worksop (Welbeck traffic)
SO	7G38	1530	Bilsthorpe
MTWO	7G39	1630	Bilsthorpe
SO	7G39	1630	Harworth
MWO	7G40	1730	Thoresby
SO	7G40	1730	Clipstone
SO	7G41	1830	Bilsthorpe
MTWO	7G41	1830	Clipstone
MTWO	7G42	1830	Kiveton Park
SuO	7G41	1930	Thoresby
SuO	7G42	2330	Bilsthorpe
MTO	7G43	2330	Worksop (Bilsthorpe traffic)
WO	7G43	2330	Clipstone

Many Nottinghamshire miners continued working during the 1984 strike and BR maintained services wherever possible. The High Marnham branch was particularly busy, and on 12 April 1984 No 56120 approaches Boughton Junction with the 7G33 empties from High Marnham to Bevercotes.

Days	Code	Arr time	From	Days	Code	Arr time	From
MO	7A21	0005	Thoresby	SuO	7A28	1310	Toton (Welbeck traffic)
TWThO	7A22	0005	Thoresby				
MO	7A22	0110	Welbeck	SX	7A29	1425	Denby
TThO	7A23	0315	Toton (Asfordby traffic)	SO	7A29	1425	Toton (Thoresby traffic)
WO	7A23	0315	Bilsthorpe	EWD	7A30	1635	Nadins
TWThO	7A24	0530	Welbeck	SuO	7A30	1710	Toton (Welbeck traffic)
FSX	7A25	0725	Toton (Thoresby traffic)	TSX	7A31	1835	Toton (Denby traffic)
MO	7A25	0910	Toton (Welbeck traffic)	TO	7A31	1835	Welbeck
MTWO	7A26	0935	Bilsthorpe	SO	7A31	1840	Welbeck
ThO	7A26	0935	Toton (Welbeck traffic)	MWO	7A32	1940	Toton (Calverton traffic)
FO	7A26	0935	Toton (Bilsthorpe traffic)	SuO	7A32	2045	Toton (Thoresby traffic)
EWD	7A27	1040	Calverton	MTWO	7A33	2300	Welbeck
MWX	7A28	1145	Nadins	SO	7A33	2310	Welbeck

Sample coal programme for Ratcliffe, September 1994

roundhouse shed at Barrow Hill managed to survive until 1991. The region's biggest marshalling complex at Toton continued to contract, although Toton locomotive depot took on increased importance as it became the base for all Class 58 and most Class 56 locomotives.

●

The privatisation of the coal, generating and railway industries in the 1990s brought sweeping changes to rail-borne coal flows in the East Midlands. National Power acquired West Burton and Willington power stations and PowerGen acquired Cottam, High Marnham, Ratcliffe and Drakelow. Both companies negotiated three-year contracts for the supply and delivery of British coal, but at the end of that period the balance was expected to shift in favour of imports. At Cottam a new east-facing curve was planned to provide a shorter route for trains of imported coal from Immingham, although as things turned out the curve was never built.

Lounge opencast disposal point opened in 1987, reached by a short spur from the Coalville line near Ashby-de-la-Zouch. Loading is under way on 24 December 1993 for the 0942 departure to Rugeley, headed by No 60077 *Canisp*. Coal loading at Lounge ceased in 1998 but the sidings remained in use as a run-round loop for trains to Hicks Lodge.

Above No 56128 heads south on the Erewash Valley line at Bennerley with an afternoon merry-go-round working for Ratcliffe on 31 July 1984. Just behind the bridge that once carried the Great Northern line to Derby Friargate is the rapid loading bunker of Bennerley opencast disposal point, built in 1983 and subsequently demolished.

Below Mining subsidence was a striking feature of the Coalville line in the 1980s. No 56064 takes the Rawdon colliery branch at Moira West Junction with empty HAAs on 28 July 1983.

Above A busy moment at Moira West Junction on 28 July 1983, as No 47229 heads an mgr train for Drakelow power station and No 56064 edges forward out of Rawdon colliery sidings. The tracks to the right gave access to Overseal sidings and the disused branch to Donisthorpe and Measham.

Left No 31302 arrives at Ollerton with the 8T19 local trip working from Mansfield Concentration Sidings on 15 June 1981. Ollerton colliery closed in 1994, and some of its reserves were then transferred to the neighbouring Thoresby pit.

Right No 20064 heads a Bolsover to Barrow Hill coal train past Seymour Junction on the evening of 27 July 1981. The semaphore signals at this location would soon be replaced under the Barrow Hill re-signalling scheme.

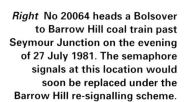

RAIL FREIGHT: COAL

The pit closures of the early 1990s included Rawdon – the last rail-served deep mine in Leicestershire – as well as Gedling, Cotgrave, Silverhill, Sherwood, Shirebrook, Bevercotes, Ollerton, Rufford, Markham, Bolsover, Shireoaks and Manton collieries in the Derbyshire/Nottinghamshire coalfield. Another rail freight loss was Avenue coking plant, which had produced both inward coal traffic in merry-go-round trains and outward wagonloads of smokeless fuel.

At some former pit locations the railway survived for other purposes, such as the Coalite plant at Bolsover and a coal stocking site at Rufford. The Cadley Hill colliery branch on the Derbyshire/Leicestershire border re-opened in 1992 to serve an opencast coal processing and disposal point known as Nadins; coal from there was transported less than 3 miles by rail to Drakelow power station. Another new opencast terminal at Doe Hill, near Alfreton, was commissioned in 1995.

Bolsover colliery and Coalite plant both produced rail traffic in the early 1990s. On 18 December 1992 No 58017 waits at the colliery loading pad while its train is loaded with coal for Ratcliffe. Several rakes of HEA wagons are visible in the Coalite sidings.

The privatised power generators rationalised their coal-fired stations in the early 1990s as new gas-fired stations came on stream. The first casualties in the East Midlands were Castle Donington and Staythorpe, while Willington power station received its 'last coal train' in July 1992, although it had its rail connection restored in the following year and remained in operation until 1999. Both High Marnham and Drakelow 'C' were seen as vulnerable but survived long enough to be sold to Eastern Group in 1995.

By 1994 almost all coal trains in the East Midlands were hauled by second-generation diesel traction – a combination of Classes 56, 58 and 60. Most workings to local power stations were diagrammed for Class 58 haulage, while long-distance services to Didcot were booked for a Class 60 and those to Brookgate and Ridham Dock in Kent were nominally Class 56-hauled. Toton consolidated its role as the biggest traction maintenance depot in the country, while the secondary depot at Shirebrook closed in favour of an expanded facility at Worksop, more conveniently situated for 1990s traffic requirements.

The division of Trainload Freight into three

Part of the Cadley Hill branch came back into use in 1992 to serve Nadins opencast disposal point. No 58016 arrives at Nadins after working 6C75, the 1255 empties from Toton, on 28 August 1992. The loaded train would run to Drakelow power station, prominent on the skyline. Traffic from Nadins finished in 1997.

companies in 1994 brought almost all East Midlands coal traffic under the control of Mainline Freight. The principal operating centres were still Toton and Worksop, but the traction was now limited to Classes 58 and 60 because the Class 56 fleet was shared between the other two companies, Transrail and Loadhaul.

Despite the ongoing programme of pit closures, the so-called super-pit at Asfordby, near Melton Mowbray, dispatched its first loaded coal train in 1991. The pit was reached by a spur from the Old Dalby test track; a proposed curve west of Melton Mowbray was never built and all trains to and from Asfordby therefore had to reverse at Melton Mowbray, generally requiring a locomotive at both ends. Initially trains ran to Rufford stocking site, but they later ran direct to Ratcliffe power station. Unfortunately Asfordby was beset with problems from the start and did not reach full production

until 1994. It was not long before 'geological problems' curtailed production again, and RJB Mining closed the multi-million-pound pit in 1997.

Further east on the Melton Mowbray line, the Castle Cement works at Ketton began receiving coal by rail in 1995 after a gap of many years. The use of MEA box wagons meant that Castle could avoid the expense of installing bottom-door discharge facilities. Between 1995 and 2005 the coal for Ketton was sourced from several different locations including Hull, Redcar, Immingham and Maltby.

●

When EWS took over the railway's bulk freight operations in 1996, just six deep mines in the East Midlands remained in operation: Calverton, Bilsthorpe, Clipstone, Thoresby and Welbeck in RJB ownership, and Bentinck owned by Coal Investments. Even those survivors were far from safe – Bilsthorpe closed in 1997 and Calverton in 1999. The closure of Calverton marked the end of coal-mining in the Leen Valley district north of Nottingham. Bentinck pit closed in 2000 and Clipstone in 2003, the latter colliery having

The would-be super-pit at Asfordby, near Melton Mowbray, had a chequered and foreshortened life. No 58050 stands at the temporary loading pad on 24 April 1992 while its 21 HAAs are loaded for the daily departure to Rufford coal stocking site. No 58046 was coupled to the other end of the train – this was standard practice in order to avoid run-round manoeuvres at the loading point and at Melton Mowbray.

survived for almost a decade after its original closure proposal by British Coal. Welbeck came close to closure in 2005 but was reprieved after the workforce agreed to adopt new procedures.

Pit closures were not necessarily the end of the story as far as branch lines were concerned. In some cases substantial coal stocks remained at the pithead, for eventual movement by rail or road. The Bevercotes branch re-opened temporarily for the removal of stockpiled coal in 1996-97, and the Gedling branch was restored at a cost of £½ million for a similar flow in 1998. However, the network of freight-only lines in Nottinghamshire and Derbyshire continued to contract, including the through line between Elmton & Creswell and Seymour, which was finally disconnected in 1998.

Opencast disposal points continued to come and go as firms had their planning permission granted and renewed for fixed periods. The long-standing terminal at Denby dispatched its last train in April 1999, leaving no further use for the 5-mile branch from Little Eaton Junction. A new opencast loading pad was provided at Renishaw in 1998 and another at Codnor Park – with the help of a £438,000 Freight Facilities Grant – in 2001. Oxcroft disposal point in Derbyshire remained active in 2005, with shunting still carried out by industrial locomotives, although its future was rumoured to be uncertain.

On the Coalville line, the former Rawdon colliery branch re-opened for six months in 1997/98 to allow the removal of surplus coal stocks. The opencast terminals at Coalfields Farm, Lounge and Nadins all closed, but new loading facilities were opened at Hicks Lodge in 1998 and at Swains Park in 2001, the latter supported by a

The Ripley branch lost its regular passenger service in 1930 but much of the branch remained open for coal from Denby until 1999. No 58004 crawls to a halt at Coxbench crossing with empty hoppers for loading at Denby on 8 July 1993. When loaded, the train will form the 1159 departure to Drakelow.

£557,100 Freight Facilities Grant. However, both Hicks Lodge and Swains Park were out of use again by 2005 – such is the unpredictability of coal movements.

The bulk of the output from East Midlands pits and opencast sites continued to head for the Trent Valley power stations. The PowerGen plant at Ratcliffe remained an important coal consumer after the commissioning of flue gas desulphurisation equipment in the 1990s. In the early 2000s it took coal from a range of deep mines and opencast sites both locally and further afield, including Thoresby, Welbeck, Oxcroft, Swains Park, Daw Mill, Butterwell and Killoch. Imported coal was conspicuous by its absence.

Cottam and West Burton power stations were acquired by EDF Energy in 2000 and 2001 respectively, and both were fitted with flue gas desulphurisation equipment in order to assure their future beyond 2008. In the early 2000s Cottam took coal mainly from English and Scottish sources, including Thoresby, Welbeck, Butterwell, Killoch and Knockshinnoch, though there were also some movements of imported coal through Immingham. Its neighbour West Burton was supplied from a similar range of sources, with some substantial movements from Hunterston deep-water port in 2002. EDF Energy reached

agreement with UK Coal in 2004 to buy between 7 and 8 million tonnes of coal over a three-year period, likely to be sourced from Welbeck, Thoresby, Harworth and Oxcroft.

High Marnham power station, dating back to 1959, was already living on borrowed time as the 21st century dawned. It received its last trainload of coal in March 2003, although the line beyond Thoresby Colliery Junction remained in use a little longer for the removal of some stockpiled coal, but was then closed for good. Drakelow 'C' power station also closed in 2003, bringing the demise of the short branch with its triangular connection from the Coalville line just south of Burton-on-Trent.

The closure of the coking and patent fuel plants at Avenue and Ollerton had left Bolsover Coalite as the only active smokeless fuel plant in Nottinghamshire. Coalite received inward trainloads of coal from Gascoigne Wood, and received a £953,000 Freight Facilities Grant in 1998 to improve its discharge and handling facilities. However, that traffic ceased in 2004, bringing the closure of the freight-only Bolsover branch. The only industrial customer in Derbyshire and Nottinghamshire receiving coal and coke by rail in 2005 was Lafarge (formerly Blue Circle Cement) at Earles Sidings in the Hope Valley.

6.

North Wales and the North West

J ust two deep mines remained in the North Wales coalfield by the mid-1970s, Bersham and Point of Ayr. Industrial steam survived at Bersham until the end of the decade; one of the last two 'industrials' based at Bersham – a 1937-built cut-down Peckett named *Hornet* – was rescued for preservation and later transferred to the Ribble Steam Railway at Preston. In later years Bersham dispatched one daily merry-go-round train to Fiddlers Ferry power station. It survived the 1984/85 miners' strike but wound its last coal

Class 24 No D5038 leaves the exchange sidings at Gresford colliery, north of Wrexham, with loaded 16-ton and 21-ton mineral wagons on 5 June 1972. At that time a large fleet of Class 24s was allocated to the Stoke Division for freight duties around Stoke, Crewe and North Wales. *Tom Heavyside*

in 1986 and was subsequently converted into a museum. The last train of stockpiled coal left the site in early 1987.

Point of Ayr colliery, situated on the coast well away from the main North Wales coalfield, also dispatched regular merry-go-round trains to Fiddlers Ferry power station. It was targeted for closure in British Coal's announcement of October 1992 but actually survived until 1996. In later years it was a drift mine, with workings extending under the sea.

The site of the long-closed Gatewen colliery near Wrexham was used for loading opencast coal intermittently in the 1970s and early 1980s, with flows operating to Rockcliffe Hall and Fiddlers Ferry power stations. After 1982 the coal from Gatewen was the only revenue-earning traffic on

The last two North Wales pits, Bersham and Point of Ayr, both sent mgr trains to Fiddlers Ferry power station in their later years. No 47192 approaches Wrexham General with 6J25, the 1345 empties from Fiddlers Ferry to Bersham, on 12 August 1982. The two signal boxes facing each other were both still in use, one for the ex-Great Western line through General and the other for the ex-Great Central line to Wrexham Exchange and Central.

the rump of the former Brymbo branch past the site of Croes Newydd yard.

Industrial coal and coke destinations in North Wales in the 1970s included the steelworks at Shotton and Brymbo, but the closure of the blast furnaces at Shotton and the complete closure of Brymbo works put an end to that traffic. However, in 1996 EWS began conveying trainloads of industrial coal to the Castle Cement works at Penyffordd, re-activating sidings that had not been used since the end of cement traffic in 1990. The coal typically ran twice weekly, but often under short-term planning arrangements, as the point of origin was liable to change at short notice. Between 1996 and 2005 Penyffordd received coal from import terminals at Redcar, Immingham, Hull, Liverpool and Avonmouth, as well as from Thoresby colliery.

●

In Lancashire, eight deep mines retained a rail connection in the mid-1970s: Cronton, Sutton Manor, Bold, Parkside, Golborne, Bickershaw, Agecroft and Hapton. By the mid-1980s that figure was reduced to two, with only Parkside and Bickershaw still sending out coal by rail. During that time span BR had also eliminated some of its antiquated operations such as trainloads of unfitted wagons to locations such as Carrington and Wyre Dock, while the NCB had finally said goodbye to steam in the North West by withdrawing its 'Austerity' 0-6-0s at Bold and Bickershaw.

The pit at Parkside was relatively new, dating back only to 1964, while Bickershaw was given a new lease of life in the 1980s with a rapid loader for merry-go-round traffic and underground links from the neighbouring Parsonage and Golborne collieries. Another source of coal traffic on the Bickershaw branch was Albert opencast disposal point, where a loading bunker was installed close to the site of the long-closed Albert colliery.

Although the opencast traffic from Albert was short-lived, Bickershaw colliery continued to dispatch large volumes of coal, all in merry-go-round trains and mostly destined for Fiddlers Ferry power station. In later years the 3-mile branch from Wigan Springs Branch to Bickershaw was

Above Industrial steam survived at Bold colliery until the early 1980s. Hunslet 0-6-0ST 'Austerity' *Whiston*, works number 3694 of 1950, seems an incongruous sight coupled to mgr wagons at Bold on 20 August 1974. *Tom Heavyside*

Right The Rawtenstall branch lost its passenger service in 1972 but survived for eight more years for traffic to Rawtenstall coal depot. No 25027 is about to depart from Rawtenstall with the empties on 20 July 1976. *Tom Heavyside*

Left With the lack of a run-round loop forcing all trains to be 'topped and tailed', the Bickershaw branch was effectively a long siding from Wigan Springs Branch. Nos 20045 and 20159 are attached to the Wigan end of a Fiddlers Ferry train at Bickershaw on the evening of 7 June 1989; two further Class 20s are attached at the rear.

unusual in having no run-round facility; trains were therefore 'topped and tailed', initially with two pairs of Class 20 locomotives and later with two Class 60s. The closure announcement for Bickershaw came in January 1992 and the last coal train ran later that year. The branch was left intact in the hope of further traffic, but none materialised.

Parkside survived just a little longer than Bickershaw, winding its last coal in October 1992; it therefore held the distinction of being the last deep mine in Lancashire. As with a number of pits closed at that time, Parkside had benefited from recent investment and had the potential to keep producing coal for many years, but British Coal was unable to sell that coal at an economic rate. The site of Parkside colliery, with its good rail and road access, was purchased by Railtrack in 1998 for a potential rail-served distribution terminal, but no physical work on that project had taken place by 2005.

The closure of older power stations such as

After the closure of Woodhead, mgr coal trains from Yorkshire to Fiddlers Ferry were re-routed via Stockport and continued to use the freight-only line to Warrington via Lymm, until that too closed in 1985. No 56020 passes over the Manchester Ship Canal on the approach to Warrington with 6M51, the 1139 from Healey Mills to Fiddlers Ferry, on 22 February 1983.

Huncoat, Chadderton and Agecroft left the 2,000MW Fiddlers Ferry station, commissioned in 1971, as the major destination for trainload coal in the industrial North West. Despite the proximity of Lancashire and North Wales pits, Fiddlers Ferry took its coal from a wide range of sources, including high tonnages from Yorkshire, which were channelled via the Woodhead route until its closure in 1981. Other locations supplying Fiddlers Ferry at that time were Wolstanton, Point of Ayr, Bersham, Bickershaw, Parkside, Bold, Haig (Whitehaven) and Maryport.

Operationally, Fiddlers Ferry suffered the handicap of being situated on the Warrington to Ditton freight-only line. Trains arriving from the north – including trans-Pennine workings after the closure of the Woodhead route – had to reverse at Walton Old Junction and again at Latchford in order to complete their journey. To reduce the time and cost of run-round movements, BR carried out trials with the 'topping and tailing' of trains by single Class 20s, and with the use of a Class 08 'drawback' locomotive; however, neither system was pursued in the EWS era. BR also proposed building a new curve at Arpley to eliminate one of the run-round movements.

A major change at Fiddlers Ferry was heralded in 1989 when BR delivered the first trainload of imported coal from Liverpool Gladstone Dock; the initial trials were successful and soon BR was

Sample coal programme for Fiddlers Ferry, April 1995

Days	Code	Arr time	From
MX	7M61	0230	Milford West
MX	7M62	0304	Milford West
MX	7T98	0805	Walton Old Junction (traffic from Milford West)
MWSO	7M52	1005	Milford West
ThFO	7T97	1230	Liverpool Bulk Terminal
MTO	7P64	1230	Warrington Arpley (traffic from Grangemouth)
SX	7M25	1530	Milford West
WFO	7F62	1630	Point of Ayr
SX	7M57	1935	Milford West

Left Having run round at Latchford sidings, Corus-liveried No 60033 *Tees Steel Express* passes Arpley Junction with coal in JMAs for Fiddlers Ferry power station on 14 February 2002.

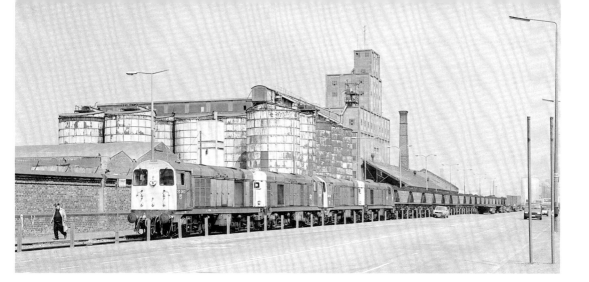

Above To cater for increased loadings of 45 HAA wagons from Liverpool Docks, BR introduced quadruple-heading with Class 20s between Gladstone Dock and Edge Hill. Nos 20052, 20187, 20128 and 20168 approach Regent Road level crossing with the second coal train of the day out of the docks on 26 May 1990. The use of four Class 20s later gave way to double-headed Class 56s.

Sample coal programme for Fiddlers Ferry, February 1997			
Days	Code	Arr time	From
MX	7P82	0030	Liverpool Bulk Terminal
EWD	7P71	0230	Liverpool Bulk Terminal
EWD	7P79	0430	Liverpool Bulk Terminal
EWD	7P74	0630	Liverpool Bulk Terminal
ThSO	7P83	0730	Walton Old Junction (traffic from Killoch)
SX	7P80	0830	Liverpool Bulk Terminal
EWD	7P72	1030	Liverpool Bulk Terminal
MWThSO	7P90	1130	Walton Old Junction (traffic from Grangemouth)
SX	7P75	1430	Liverpool Bulk Terminal
EWD	7P77	1230	Liverpool Bulk Terminal
SX	7P81	1630	Liverpool Bulk Terminal
SO	7F60	1645	Carlisle London Road
SX	7P73	1830	Liverpool Bulk Terminal
SX	7P78	2030	Liverpool Bulk Terminal
SX	7P76	2230	Liverpool Bulk Terminal

Right Although intended for Fiddlers Ferry traffic, Liverpool Bulk Terminal forwarded coal to other locations, including Horrocksford cement works at Clitheroe. No 66014 draws forward with MEA wagons ready to form 6P82, the 1430 from Liverpool to Clitheroe, on 1 June 1999.

running up to seven trains a day from Liverpool to Fiddlers Ferry. Train lengths were increased from 27 to 45 merry-go-round wagons to make the operation more efficient; however, this also meant quadruple-heading with Class 20s on the steeply graded section from Gladstone Dock to Edge Hill until more powerful traction became available. An alternative loading point at Bidston, across the Mersey estuary, was tried in 1988 but did not become established.

Once it became clear that imported coal was here to stay, PowerGen decided to invest some £40 million in a purpose-built rapid loading terminal at Gladstone Dock, capable of handling up to 5 million tonnes of coal a year. The new facility, usually known as Liverpool Bulk Terminal (LBT), came into use in August 1993. BR also upgraded the track and signalling on the freight-only docks branch, including the restoration of double track between Bootle and Regent Road level crossing.

Traffic volumes from LBT were lower than anticipated in the early years, partly because PowerGen was generating less electricity from its coal-fired plants and partly because Fiddlers Ferry was still receiving coal from other sources, including Yorkshire collieries via Milford West sidings. However, some extra business for LBT came in the shape of short-term movements to Cottam power station, also owned by PowerGen.

By the late 1990s Fiddlers Ferry was receiving its coal mainly from LBT, although supplies also arrived from Hunterston port and from Scottish opencast sources such as Knockshinnoch, Killoch and Ayr Harbour. The Liverpool to Fiddlers Ferry circuit meanwhile became home to the former National Power blue-liveried bogie hopper wagons. The power station itself changed hands three times: from PowerGen to Edison Mission Energy in 1999, to American Electric Power in 2001, and to Scottish & Southern Energy in 2004.

Alongside the Fiddlers Ferry traffic, LBT handled short-term coal flows to Ironbridge power station and to Castle Cement at Penyffordd and Clitheroe. The combination of more frequent coal trains and increasing scrap metal traffic for European Metals Recycling made the freight-only branch from Edge Hill to Liverpool Docks busier than it had been for several decades. Plans were made to re-instate the curve between Olive Mount Junction and Edge Lane Junction, which would eliminate the need for all trains to reverse; however, that proposal remained on the drawing-board in 2005.

Before the development of Gladstone Dock, Liverpool was associated with coal exports for Ireland rather than with imports. The main export location was Garston, where a huge fan of sidings once accommodated hundreds of loose-coupled mineral wagons waiting to discharge their load. The BR timetable of 1972/73 shows numerous

Freight returned to Ellesmere Port in 2005 when Freightliner Heavy Haul won a contract to supply Fiddlers Ferry with imported coal from Manisty Wharf, Ellesmere Port. The coal reached the UK at Hunterston and was conveyed by coastal shipping from Hunterston to Ellesmere Port – evidently a more cost-effective option than moving the coal by train from Hunterston to Fiddlers Ferry. Nos 66616 and 66610 cause mild excitement at Ellesmere Port station as they arrive with 4F03, the 1515 empties from Fiddlers Ferry, on 2 August 2005. FHH provided two locomotives in the early days of the contract to overcome wheel slip problems on the tightly curved Manisty Wharf branch.

The export coal traffic to Garston benefited from mgr wagons in its last years. No 58029 passes Garston Church Road box with the 6L31 empties from the docks on 2 April 1986.

Class 9, ie unfitted, trains reaching Garston from locations such as Toton, Mansfield, Wath, Rotherwood and Tinsley.

BR later modernised its operation at Garston and introduced HBA manual-discharge hopper wagons, until they in turn were replaced by merry-go-round stock. The points of origin in the 1980s included Three Spires Junction, Mansfield Concentration Sidings and Bestwood Park. However, Garston coal terminal closed completely in 1991, with the remaining export business for Ireland being carried in Cawoods containers and offloaded at Ellesmere Port. That operation in turn was transferred to Seaforth in 1992.

Industrial coal to the Brunner Mond chemical works at Winnington and Lostock, near Northwich, remained on rail until the company replaced its coal-fired boilers with a gas-fired Combined Heat and Power plant in 2000. In later years Winnington took coal in merry-go-round hoppers from Killoch, and Lostock received its supplies in MEA wagons from Redcar.

●

A surprising revival in East Lancashire was the resumption of coal traffic to Padiham power station in November 1991. The station had last received coal by rail in the 1970s, although the Padiham branch had remained open to handle occasional trainloads of fuel oil for the initial firing up of the power station's boilers. As there were no hopper discharge facilities at Padiham, BR carried

the new coal traffic in open box wagons hired from NACCO. Those wagons had previously carried aggregates – an interesting reversal of the situation that often occurred in the 1980s when former coal wagons found themselves drafted into aggregates flows. The coal originated at Maryport opencast disposal point and was conveyed in a daily Class 60-hauled train. Unfortunately the traffic lasted only until 1993, when the power station closed. The railway's final act at Padiham was to remove surplus stockpiled coal from the site, with merry-go-round trains destined for Rugeley power station.

Rail freight returned to the Clitheroe line in 1997 when EWS started delivering coal to the Castle Cement works at Horrocksford. In the early days the coal came from various locations including Redcar import terminal and Maltby colliery. The loaded trains were routed via Healey Mills, Leeds and Hellifield, with reversals at Healey Mills and Hellifield – quite a circuitous route, which reflected traincrew needs and allowed the trains to reverse into the siding at Horrocksford. The routeing was later switched to Hebden Bridge and Blackburn, with trains entering the Horrocksford works directly from the south. Other points of origin included Immingham, Hull and Liverpool import terminals. However, Horrocksford stopped taking coal by rail in 2005 when it increased its use of alternative fuels, including 'agricultural waste derived fuel' derived from sterilised abattoir waste, for its

Above No 40129 arrives at Lakeland opencast disposal point, Maryport, with 6P49, the 0655 mgr empties from Workington, on 13 July 1983. At that time Maryport sent a daily train to Fiddlers Ferry and local trips as required to Workington Docks, while Haig colliery at Whitehaven sent coal to Fiddlers Ferry and Northwich.

Below Coal from Maryport was delivered by rail to Workington Docks for export. No 47372 draws its rake of 30 HAAs through the discharge hopper house before returning to Maryport for a second trip on 30 July 1985.

Padiham received its first coal train for a decade on 16 November 1991, when BR hired open box wagons from NACCO to fulfil a contract with National Power. No 60032 waits while the mechanical grab empties the first half of its train. On the left is the oil discharge terminal that had kept the Padiham branch active in the 1980s.

modern dry-process kiln, and closed its two older wet-process kilns.

The small coalfield on the Cumbrian coast was largely worked out by the 1970s. The last deep mine in the area, Haig colliery near Whitehaven, once produced coking coal for Workington steelworks, but by the early 1980s its output was mainly steam coal for Fiddlers Ferry power station. It closed in 1986 in the wake of the miners' strike, leaving the opencast terminal at Maryport as the only rail-borne coal source in Cumbria. Maryport was equipped with a rapid loading bunker and dispatched merry-go-round trains to Workington Docks for export as well as to Fiddlers Ferry. By the early 1990s the Workington traffic had ceased, but Maryport continued to send coal to English power stations, including the short-term flow to Padiham mentioned above, until its closure in 1993. After that, an opencast coal loading point was established at Carlisle London Road, remaining in operation until the early 2000s.

Colliery steam survived in many parts of the country into and beyond 1968. One of the less well-known haunts was Whitehaven, where NCB locomotives ferried wagons to and from the BR exchange sidings. Robert Stephenson & Hawthorns 0-4-0ST works number 7049 is pictured with empty 21-ton hoppers at Whitehaven Harbour on 20 June 1968. *Michael Mensing*

7.

Yorkshire

Not so long ago, coal mines seemed a permanent feature of the industrial landscape across a huge swathe of Yorkshire, from Leeds and Selby in the north to Sheffield and the Nottinghamshire border in the south. The focus of mining had gradually shifted from the shallow seams on the Pennine fringe in the west towards the deeper seams in the east of the region. However, some of the older pits in the west, such as Emley Moor and Dodworth, remained in production until the early 1980s. Meanwhile the ambitious Selby coalfield development of the 1980s failed to live up to expectations and its last coal was brought to the surface in 2004.

The trickle of Yorkshire pit closures in the late 1960s and early 1970s was overshadowed by the revolution in the generating industry brought about by the opening of three new CEGB stations in the Aire Valley: Ferrybridge 'C', Eggborough and Drax. Together they became the focus for one

of the most intensive freight operations in the country, moving around 300,000 tonnes of coal a week from a total of around 30 collieries. The BR diesel depot at Knottingley was opened in 1966 with the new Aire Valley traffic in mind, and as early as 1973 the railway introduced a computerised timetabling system – known as Airepower – to ensure the efficient deployment of up to 13 locomotives and 45 Knottingley traincrews.

The Airepower system predated BR's nationwide Total Operations Processing System (TOPS) of the late 1970s and relied on data being transmitted down a telephone line from BR's Leeds divisional office to its ICL 1904A computer at Crewe. Each Thursday morning BR received details of the CEGB's requirements at Ferrybridge, Eggborough and Drax in terms of colliery and tonnage, and within 3 hours Airepower produced a draft merry-go-round trainplan, taking account

Glasshoughton coking plant is pictured on 21 August 1974, with No 31209 passing on the main line and Hawthorn Leslie 0-6-0 saddle tank *Coal Products No 3* (works number 3575) shunting 16-ton mineral wagons. The site of Glasshoughton colliery and coking plant has since been redeveloped as a massive retail and leisure centre, while the saddle tank survives at the time of writing on the Tanfield Railway.
Tom Heavyside

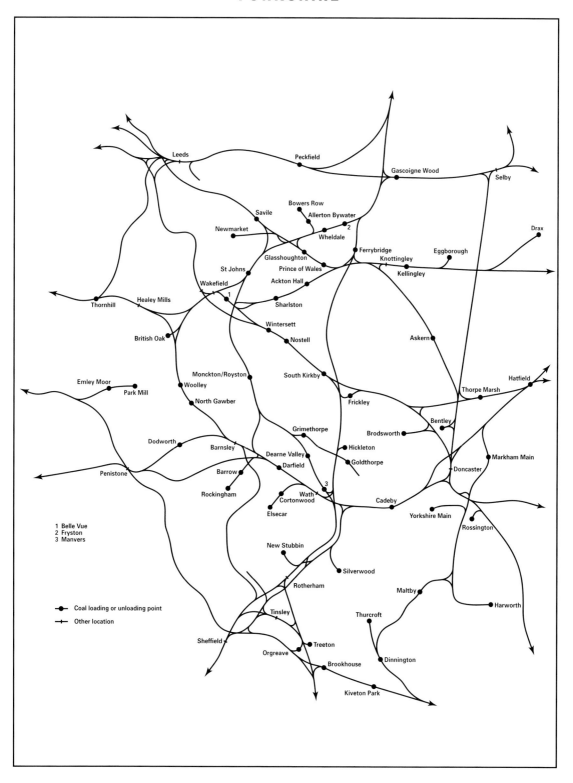

Yorkshire railways in the late 1970s, showing coal loading and unloading points.

of practical constraints such as terminal layout, terminal opening hours, signal box opening hours, and suitable locations for the traincrew to take physical needs breaks.

With an average distance from pithead to power station of only around 15 miles, Airepower made it possible to achieve up to six or seven loaded journeys a day for a single locomotive and wagon set – a phenomenal improvement on what had been possible a few years earlier with loose-coupled wagons and manual planning. The older power station at Thorpe Marsh was excluded from Airepower, even though it could take coal in merry-go-round hopper wagons.

The normal traction for many Yorkshire merry-go-round trains in the 1970s was the Class 47. The

standard train length was 30 wagons – rather short by 21st century standards, but the maximum that could be hauled comfortably by a Class 47 on some routes in the region. In 1980 Knottingley received its quota of Class 56s, which enabled a modest but worthwhile increase in train length to 34 wagons. The 56s were to remain a familiar sight on Yorkshire coal duties for more than two decades.

Although a large proportion of Yorkshire coal was moving in merry-go-round trains, BR still operated older-style vacuum-braked and unfitted coal wagons on some trainload flows until the early 1980s. They included Park Mill colliery (Clayton West) to Elland, Wath to Keadby, Monckton coking plant to Northwich, and Orgreave coking plant to Scunthorpe. The former

No 47038 leaves Dodworth colliery on 28 March 1974 with a trip working to Barnsley Junction, Penistone, where it will be combined with another portion for the trunk haul to Fiddlers Ferry power station. *Tom Heavyside*

Class 56 locomotives took over from Class 47s on Aire Valley mgr workings around 1980. No 56034 takes the Castleford line at Burton Salmon with a loaded train for Ferrybridge on 11 August 1981. Receding towards York are Nos 31188 and 31409 with the Tilcon roadstone train to Hull.

The network of colliery lines in the Barnsley area gradually closed down as seams became worked out or uneconomic. One of the last survivors was Barrow colliery, reached by a spur from the former Great Central Barnsley-Sheffield line. Nos 20029 and 20031 leave the exchange sidings for Barrow with a Class 9 trip working to Wath on 4 March 1981.

Great Central marshalling yard at Wath was still a gathering point for coal mined in the Barnsley area, although its importance declined as the number of local pits shrank – from more than 40 when the yard opened in 1907/08 to less than ten by the late 1970s.

The decade of the 1980s began with one of the most controversial railway closures of the post-Beeching era – the trans-Pennine Woodhead route with its three Yorkshire tentacles serving Wath, Tinsley and Rotherwood. Although Woodhead boasted the newest main-line railway tunnel in the country and a generous loading gauge, its non-standard electrification system and ageing Class 76 locomotives were in need of major refurbishment or renewal, and it was difficult to justify such expenditure when the level of trans-Pennine freight traffic was continuing to fall. Many loaded trains required not only double-heading but also banking assistance on the Worsborough incline from Wombwell to West Silkstone Junction, which added substantially to the line's day-to-day operating costs.

After the axe fell on Woodhead on 18 July 1981, it was a relatively straightforward matter to re-route the remaining trans-Pennine flows. The Fiddlers Ferry coal trains were diverted via Healey Mills yard and Hebden Bridge with little adverse effect on overall journey times. An exception was the flow from Dodworth colliery near Penistone, which faced a long diversion via Wath and Healey Mills, but that traffic was soon to cease with the opening of an underground link from Dodworth to Woolley. One of the benefits of the Woodhead closure was that trains no longer had to stop for a

Class 31 No 5560, soon to be renumbered 31142, approaches the reception sidings at Tinsley yard with empty 16-ton mineral wagons on 15 May 1972. One of Tinsley's three Class 13 'master and slave' shunters propels SPV plate wagons over the hump. Visible in the background is a rake of HCO coke hopper wagons, likely to have been used on the Orgreave-Scunthorpe circuit. *J. H. Cooper-Smith*

Above Most trans-Pennine coal trains via Woodhead had to negotiate the Worsborough incline, which included a 2¼-mile stretch with a ruling gradient of 1 in 40. Merry-go-round trains required banking from Wombwell to West Silkstone Junction. Nos 76034 and 76032 approach West Silkstone Junction with a Wath to Fiddlers Ferry working on 18 June 1981; here the bankers would be detached and Nos 76034 and 76032 would continue unaided to Godley Junction.

Below 'Tommy' electrics Nos 76039 and 76037 enter the disused Dunford Bridge station on 8 January 1981 with 8M29, the 0325 from Mansfield Concentration Sidings to Garston Docks. This service was one of several daily trains conveying coal for export to Ireland. The MCV and MCO wagons would soon be replaced by air-braked HBA hoppers, until they in turn gave way to HAA hoppers.

Above The huge Manvers coal and coke complex dominates the skyline as No 37120 heads east on the former Great Central line from Wath to Mexborough with empty mineral wagons on 28 March 1977. This line closed in the 1980s, as did the former Midland Railway line that can be seen curving round in the middle of the picture and the Manvers complex itself. *Gavin Morrison*

traction change at Godley Junction on the west side of the Pennines.

The remaining railway infrastructure around Wath gradually became superfluous as sources of traffic dried up. The line from Wath to Barnsley shut in 1985 and the demise of Manvers colliery and coking plant in 1988/89 left no further use for the surviving connections from Wath Central Junction to Mexborough and Dearne Junction. The area once occupied by Wath yard had become

The rapid loader for Goldthorpe colliery kept a short stretch of the former Dearne Valley Railway alive, reached by a spur from the Swinton & Knottingley Joint Line at Hickleton. No 56081 arrives at Goldthorpe on 20 April 1993 before forming 7K89, the 1602 mgr service to Ferrybridge power station. Goldthorpe wound its last coal in 1994.

a wasteland by 2004, flanked by the new A6023 road.

Elsewhere in the region, pit closures caused the railway system to contract year by year. Three

No 40074 sets out from Fryston colliery towards Castleford with a loaded coal train on 10 September 1981. A varied selection of internal and BR wagons can be seen in the colliery sidings. The colliery closed in 1985 and the signal box was decommissioned two years later. *Dr L. A. Nixon*

miles of the former Dearne Valley Railway from Cudworth to Hickleton closed in 1978 when BR opened a new connection with the Moorthorpe to Sheffield line at Hickleton. The end of coal winding at Emley Moor and Park Mill collieries on the Clayton West branch was doubtless a factor in the decision to withdraw the passenger service on that branch – thereby closing it completely – in 1983. The former Midland Railway main line from Houghton Main to Wath Road Junction closed in 1987, having already lost most of its passenger traffic four years previously.

It was the NCB's announcement on 5 March 1984 that Cortonwood pit, near Barnsley, was to close that sparked the miners' strike of 1984/85. Within a few days more than half of Britain's miners had downed their tools and the bitterest and longest industrial dispute of the late 20th century had begun. Another Yorkshire location, Orgreave coking plant near Sheffield, became the scene of major clashes during the strike. But the biggest effect of that strike in Yorkshire was the accelerated programme of pit closures, totalling seven – including Cortonwood – in 1985, four in 1986, four in 1987, two in 1988 and three in 1989.

Offering some temporary compensation for the pit closures was the development of the Selby coalfield, heralded in the 1970s as the largest deep coal mine project ever undertaken in the world. The site covered more than 100 square miles and involved the sinking of ten shafts. One of its consequences would be the re-routeing of the East

The Selby mine complex produced large quantities of spoil, which from September 1990 were conveyed by rail to a purpose-built discharge terminal at Welbeck, near the site of St John's colliery. At its height the traffic amounted to five 47-wagon trains a day, each carrying around 1,500 tonnes of spoil. No 56088 departs from Welbeck with empties for Gascoigne Wood on 25 October 1991.

Coast Main Line to avoid subsidence on the historic route between Selby and York. Elaborate coal loading facilities were constructed on a former marshalling yard site at Gascoigne Wood, with two overhead bunkers for coal and a third for colliery waste, which would be conveyed by rail to Welbeck landfill site near Normanton. The site also housed a rail discharge terminal for incoming coal from other collieries, used to 'sweeten' the Selby coal to make it more suitable for the end user.

The first coal emerged from Wistow mine, one of the five collieries that made up the Selby complex, in July 1983. Within a year production was halted by the miners' strike, but it resumed in 1985 and soon reached a climax of more than 30 merry-go-round departures each weekday with additional trains at weekends. Most of the coal was destined for Drax; the short distances and efficient handling at both ends of the route meant that a single train could complete four circuits between Gascoigne Wood and Drax in a 14-hour period. Other destinations reached from Gascoigne Wood included Eggborough, Ferrybridge and Fiddlers Ferry power stations and the Coalite plant at Bolsover.

●

The huge steel-making complex at Scunthorpe received trainloads of coal and coke from British sources until the late 1980s, the British Steel Corporation having invested in an mgr discharge terminal there in 1977. The coal came from a range of collieries including Oakdale in South Wales, Betteshanger in Kent, Wolstanton in Staffordshire, and local pits such as Dinnington

and Silverwood. Several trains a day brought coke from Orgreave.

However, in 1989 British Steel switched to overseas coal and opened its own import terminal at Immingham, located adjacent to the existing ore terminal. Scunthorpe was soon receiving up to six trains of coal a day from Immingham, as well as smaller volumes from Thurcroft and other British pits. By 2002 the number of coal trains on the Immingham-Scunthorpe circuit had reached ten per day; however, the switch to HTA wagons in 2003 enabled an increase in payload per train and therefore a reduction in the number of trains. Scunthorpe also received trainloads of coke from Redcar in HEA hopper wagons – one of the few traffic flows still using that wagon type in 2005.

Other industrial coal consumers in Yorkshire included coking plants at Askern, Manvers, Smithywood, Monckton, Orgreave and Grimethorpe; the Grimethorpe plant continued to generate inward coal and outward Coalite movements by rail until its closure in the mid-1990s.

Until the 1980s Immingham was a key export location for British-mined coal, using the NCB hopper discharge terminal that had opened in 1971. The throughput at the NCB terminal reached 26 booked arrivals each weekday by 1983, originating at various yards, collieries and coking plants including Doncaster, Healey Mills, Worksop, Thoresby, North Gawber, Avenue and Manvers. That traffic declined sharply after the miners' strike and the NCB terminal eventually switched to handling imports instead of exports.

●

In the early 1980s large quantities of coal were exported through Immingham, using the NCB's own mgr discharge terminal. On 12 April 1983 No 56112 passes Barnetby with 6L56, the 1204 from Immingham to Healey Mills. Twenty years later, the same wagon type could be seen carrying coal in the opposite direction.

RAIL FREIGHT: COAL

Coal traffic patterns in Yorkshire in the 1990s were shaped by the continuing decline of the Yorkshire coalfield and by the trend towards using opencast and imported coal. The British Coal closure list of October 1992 condemned 11 Yorkshire pits: Sharlston, Prince of Wales, Grimethorpe, Houghton Main, Frickley, Bentley, Hatfield, Rossington, Markham Main, Maltby and Kiveton Park.

As things turned out, only three of those pits – Sharlston, Grimethorpe and Houghton Main – closed directly after the announcement, while the others were either mothballed or reprieved. However, the market conditions, especially in the generating industry, made it increasingly difficult for British Coal and its private successor, RJB

Mining, to keep the survivors in business. Bentley and Frickley closed in 1993, Kiveton Park in 1994, and Prince of Wales in 2002. Markham Main was leased to Coal Investments but closed in 1996, while Hatfield also passed into independent ownership but wound its last coal in 2004. Plans to build a coal-fired electricity generator at Hatfield, fed directly by the colliery, might have kept the pit going for another decade but were not pursued. From the list of pits reprieved in 1992, only Rossington and Maltby survived into 2005.

Perhaps the saddest mining loss in Yorkshire was the premature closure of the Selby coalfield, leading to the end of high-volume rail traffic from Gascoigne Wood. By 2000 coal was no longer mined at two of the Selby mines – Whitemoor and

Left For many years Class 47s were the preferred traction on Yorkshire merry-go-round trains. No 47291 winds out of Hatfield colliery with a train for one of the Aire Valley power stations on 5 June 1980.

Below Class 58 locomotives appeared on Yorkshire coal trains in the early 1990s, but left the region when the class was allocated en bloc to Mainline Freight in 1994. No 58041 is ready to leave Bentley colliery with 7K80, the 1210 service to Eggborough, on 20 April 1993.

Kiveton Park colliery was listed for closure in British Coal's 1992 announcement but was one of several pits to gain a short-term reprieve. No 56009 is pictured at Kiveton Park while its mgr train is loaded by mechanical grab on 29 October 1992. The colliery eventually closed in 1994.

RAIL FREIGHT: COAL

North Selby – and the annual output from the remaining three mines had declined to less than 5 million tonnes. In 2002 UK Coal announced its intention to close the complex completely and the once intensive schedule of coal trains to Drax and elsewhere gradually reduced to a trickle. The last fully laden train left Gascoigne Wood on 19 November 2004, bringing one of Britain's most modern and highly automated rail freight operations to an abrupt and untimely end. In December 2005 EWS returned the sidings at Gascoigne Wood to use as a staging and stabling location for long-distance coal traffic, relieving the burden on nearby Milford sidings.

In addition to Rossington and Maltby, the railway still carried coal from two other Yorkshire pits in 2005, Kellingley and Harworth. Situated in the Aire Valley only a few miles from Drax power station, Kellingley wound its first coal as recently as 1965 and still had substantial reserves when British Coal passed into the private sector 30 years later. However, geological problems ominously reduced its output in 2005 and it was unable to supply the expected tonnage to Drax. Harworth colliery – strictly speaking in Nottinghamshire, but situated only a few miles from Doncaster and therefore often considered to be a Yorkshire pit – started production just after the First World War and still had large untapped reserves in 2005. However UK Coal announced its intention to mothball both Harworth and Rossington in late 2005.

Yorkshire produced relatively little opencast coal traffic in the 1990s. An overhead bunker was installed at Wintersett for traffic from Anglers site, and loading took place on the re-opened Allerton Bywater branch for a short time in the early 1990s. Two opencast loading points came into temporary use in the 2000s, at Rotherham Steel Terminal and Hunslet East. The Hunslet East traffic was destined for West Burton and was unusual in that the gradient on the branch from Hunslet East to Neville Hill necessitated Class 60 haulage.

●

Movements of imported coal for the generating industry increased dramatically during the 1990s, following the first trial loads from Hull to West Burton in September 1991. A government Section 8 grant helped to provide a new pad loading facility at Hull King George Dock in the following year, and coal was conveyed from Hull to cement works such as Rugby and Foxton and, later, to power stations in the Aire and Trent Valleys. Some short-term movements also operated from New Holland, a location that had seen no rail freight for many years.

A stretch of the former Castleford to Garforth line remained in use until the 1990s to serve collieries and opencast workings. Ledston station had closed to passengers in 1951 but was still in good condition when No 47089 was photographed leaving Allerton Bywater colliery with the 8K20 trip working to Healey Mills on 15 July 1983. The signal box was to survive, remarkably, until 1988.

Right No 60093 waits for a clear exit from the Hunslet East branch at Neville Hill while heading 6B27, the 1042 mgr service from Hunslet to West Burton, on 7 April 2005. This short-term flow was the first coal to be loaded in the Leeds area since the closure of Rothwell and Belle Isle collieries in the 1970s.

Below right Why go to the expense of a rapid loading bunker when a team of mechanical grab operators can do the job just as quickly? A rake of Freightliner Heavy Haul hoppers is loaded at Hull Coal Terminal on 1 August 2005. With up to seven shovels operating simultaneously and carrying up to 9 tonnes of coal in each lift, a whole train can be loaded in as little as 40 minutes.

Below No 65545 leaves Hull Coal Terminal on the same day with 19 loaded HHA hoppers forming 6Y56, the 1445 to Drax. On that day the terminal dispatched a not unusual total of seven coal trains – five for EWS and two for Freightliner Heavy Haul.

But it was the port of Immingham that saw the biggest growth in imported coal traffic. In the late 1990s Immingham started sending trainloads of industrial coal to cement works such as Hope and Penyffordd, and from 2001 there was substantial traffic to power stations in the Aire and Trent Valleys – especially Eggborough, Ferrybridge, Cottam, West Burton and Rugeley. Loading was carried out at four locations: the Corus coal terminal (mainly at night when there were no trains to Scunthorpe); a loading pad alongside Immingham reception sidings; and two pads alongside the track formerly used by NCB export traffic.

The coal loading facilities at Immingham were further enhanced in 2002 when Associated British Ports opened a new siding serving Humber International Terminal, capable of handling more than 100 trains a week. Humber International Terminal itself is a deep-water multi-purpose terminal built alongside reclaimed land in the Humber estuary. Phase One of the terminal,

completed in 2000, provided a 300m berth capable of accepting vessels carrying up to 100,000 tonnes of cargo, supported by three 100-tonne-capacity mobile harbour cranes. In 2005 ABP announced a £44.5 million Phase Two extension, later augmented by £15 million for a second coal stacker reclaimer and ancillary equipment following the signing of a new agreement with Scottish & Southern Energy.

Despite the major shift from exports to imports, one flow of home-produced coal continued to operate to Immingham in 2005: two or three weekly trainloads of anthracite duff from Coedbach washery for the Coal Products Limited briquetting plant at the east end of Immingham reception sidings. This traffic switched from containers to merry-go-round hopper wagons in 1997 after Coal Products installed bottom-door discharge equipment. EWS later experimented with re-loading the hopper wagons with imported coal for the Midlands and South Wales in order to reduce the empty wagon mileage.

●

In the generating industry, the 1,000MW Thorpe Marsh power station near Doncaster closed in

Freightliner Heavy Haul No 66512 runs round its rake of HHA wagons at Immingham NCB siding on 7 August 2002, having arrived as the 4G35 empties from Cottam.

March 1994, having received its last rail-borne coal in the previous year. However, the railway was later contracted to remove surplus stockpiled coal from Thorpe Marsh to Drax. Meanwhile the remaining trio of power stations in the Aire Valley – Drax, Eggborough and Ferrybridge – continued to dominate the rail freight scene in the Knottingley area.

Aire Valley coal programme: a sample week in late 1993

Arrivals at Drax

Point of origin	Time	Days run
Gascoigne Wood	0036	SX + SuO
Thoresby	0136	SX
Gascoigne Wood	0206	EWD
Gascoigne Wood	0251	SuO
Gascoigne Wood	0336	EWD
Gascoigne Wood	0401	SuO
Gascoigne Wood	0416	MX
Blindwells	0456	MX
Gascoigne Wood	0511	SuO
Gascoigne Wood	0536	EWD
Thoresby	0611	WThFO
Gascoigne Wood	0616	SuO
Gascoigne Wood	0636	MX
Gascoigne Wood	0706	EWD
Gascoigne Wood	0736	SuO
Welbeck	0806	MX
Gascoigne Wood	0836	MO + SuO
Gascoigne Wood	0906	EWD
Gascoigne Wood	0931	SuO
Gascoigne Wood	1026	EWD
Gascoigne Wood	1051	SuO
Welbeck	1106	MX
Gascoigne Wood	1206	EWD
Gascoigne Wood	1211	SuO
Thoresby	1236	SX
Gascoigne Wood	1336	SX
Gascoigne Wood	1406	SuO
Gascoigne Wood	1436	SX
Gascoigne Wood	1536	SuO
Gascoigne Wood	1540	SX
Gascoigne Wood	1606	SO
Gascoigne Wood	1636	SuO
Thoresby	1638	SX
Gascoigne Wood	1706	SX
Welbeck	1736	SX + SuO
Gascoigne Wood	1751	SO
Gascoigne Wood	1838	SX
Gascoigne Wood	1906	SX + SuO

Point of origin	Time	Days run
Gascoigne Wood	1931	SO
Gascoigne Wood	2006	SX + SuO
Gascoigne Wood	2106	SX + SuO
Ellington	2136	WThFO
Gascoigne Wood	2206	SX
Gascoigne Wood	2236	SX + SuO
Gascoigne Wood	2246	SO
Gascoigne Wood	2336	SX + SuO

Arrivals at Eggborough

Point of origin	Time	Days run
Gascoigne Wood	0058	MX
Gascoigne Wood	0134	MO
Gascoigne Wood	0216	MX
Harworth	0323	MX
Prince of Wales	0913	WThFO
Sharlston	1115	SX
Gascoigne Wood	1227	SX
Gascoigne Wood	1557	SX
Prince of Wales	1623	SuO
Wearmouth	1803	SX
Gascoigne Wood	1927	SuO
Gascoigne Wood	2027	WThFO
Wearmouth	2103	MTO
Prince of Wales	2230	SuO

Arrivals at Ferrybridge

Point of origin	Time	Days run
Wardley	0115	MTO
Wearmouth	0115	WThFO
Kellingley	0241	WThFO
Goldthorpe	0425	TO
Goldthorpe	1511	MTWO
Frickley	1511	ThFO
Gascoigne Wood	1631	SX
Gascoigne Wood	1731	SX
Frickley	1947	SX
Goldthorpe	2149	SX
Gascoigne Wood	2304	SX

The rail freight potential of Drax – Western Europe's biggest coal-fired power station with a nominal output of 4,000MW – increased in the 1990s with the commissioning of flue gas desulphurisation (fgd) equipment to cut harmful emissions of sulphur dioxide from the power station. At that time Drax supplied more than 20% of National Power's output and the fitting of fgd equipment to that one plant would enable National Power to fulfil its national obligation for reducing emissions.

In railway terms, the fitting of fgd equipment to Drax was significant not just because it lengthened the life expectancy of one of rail freight's biggest destinations but also because it involved the delivery of limestone and the removal of desulphogypsum by rail. To cater for the new traffic National Power installed about 3 miles of new track, including a new approach line and a run-round facility. A two-track terminal was provided for discharging the limestone from hopper wagons and for top-loading containers with gypsum.

However, the developments at Drax were no assurance of extra traffic for BR, nor for its post-1994 successor Loadhaul. Quite apart from National Power's plans to build a conveyor belt from the Selby coalfield to Drax, which would have deprived the railway of a huge slice of its lucrative coal carryings, National Power decided to use its own locomotive on the limestone traffic from Tunstead, as a precursor to setting up its own open access operation. After a short period of operation with a BR Class 60 locomotive and hired Tiphook wagons, No 59201 duly entered service in 1994 with a rake of National Power JHA hopper wagons, and the company opened its own maintenance depot at Ferrybridge.

National Power became an open access operator in its own right after acquiring five more Class 59 locomotives and a total of 85 JMA hopper wagons for coal traffic in 1995/96. Its investment was justified partly to reduce day-to-day running costs, with an anticipated saving of £30 million over two years, and partly to increase the security of supply, with less potential for disruption caused by industrial action among railway staff.

Although National Power's open access aspirations were dogged by obstacles, not least of which were the difficulties of obtaining third party insurance cover and of satisfying Railtrack's Safety and Standards Directorate, the company was determined to achieve its aim and hoped in the longer term to run all its own trains, with a potential follow-up order for 15 more Class 59 locomotives and 415 wagons.

However, changes in both the rail freight and generating industries overtook those plans and EWS took over all National Power's railway assets in April 1998. The Class 59 locomotives found themselves redeployed on aggregates traffic in the South of England, while the coal wagons were transferred to the Liverpool-Fiddlers Ferry circuit. EWS mothballed National Power's Ferrybridge maintenance depot.

Freshly repainted in Loadhaul black and orange but without its bodyside logo, No 56034 *Castell Ogwr/Ogmore Castle* crawls forward with its mgr train at Drax on 26 August 1994. At that time Drax took about 20 trains a day from the Selby coalfield, together with a handful of deliveries from other collieries in Yorkshire and Nottinghamshire. A typical mgr train payload of 1,170 tonnes would keep one power station boiler going for about 4 hours.

Above National Power sold its Class 59 locomotives and wagon fleet to EWS in April 1998. The Class 59s were quickly repainted into EWS livery, but the wagons simply had their National Power logo painted out. No 59206 departs from Gascoigne Wood with a train for Drax on 7 August 1998. The ex-National Power Class 59s were later transferred to the London area, while the JMA wagons were redeployed on the Liverpool-Fiddlers Ferry flow.

Below Despite competition from Freightliner Heavy Haul, EWS retained a large slice of the coal traffic to Aire Valley power stations and made increasing use of its new HTA wagons. No 66243 passes Milford Junction with coal from Gascoigne Wood to Drax on 24 April 2001.

Drax power station was sold to the American corporation AES in 1999 and became an independent generating company, trading under the name of Drax Power Limited, in 2003. A five-year deal for the supply of up to 14 million tonnes of British-mined coal was signed with UK Coal in 2004; however, the power station continued to receive opencast coal from Scotland and imported coal alongside deliveries from collieries such as Kellingley, Maltby and Daw Mill. In 2004 Drax Power Limited received permission to burn a mixture of petroleum coke and coal in one of its six generating units for a trial period of 18 months; the petroleum coke was expected to be delivered by rail.

The 2,000MW Eggborough power station was sold by National Power to British Energy – already the owner of eight nuclear power stations in England and Scotland – in 2000. British Energy decided to install flue gas desulphurisation equipment to two of Eggborough's four generating units, with full commissioning planned for 2005. In the meantime Eggborough had switched from consuming locally mined coal to using mainly low-sulphur imported and Scottish opencast coal. The

sources in 2004/05 included Immingham, New Cumnock, Knockshinnoch, Killoch and Ravenstruther.

Ferrybridge 'C' power station was sold by PowerGen to Edison Mission Energy in 1999, to American Electric Power in 2001, and to Scottish & Southern Energy in 2004. The 2,000MW facility was taking imported coal by rail from various sources in 2005, including Redcar, Immingham, Hull and Hunterston. In the past it had received much of its coal by barge from Kellingley colliery, using the Aire & Calder Navigation. Ferrybridge was a good example of a customer producing much longer-distance rail traffic because of the decline of the British coal industry.

The trend towards unloading by mechanical grab, rather than using hopper discharge, was reflected in EWS's growing fleet of two-axle MEA and bogie MBA open box wagons. No 60100 departs from Healey Mills with 6Z98, the 0130 service from Maltby to Clitheroe, on 26 August 1998. This train followed a circuitous route via Healey Mills (reverse), Normanton, Shipley and Hellifield (reverse).

8.

The North East

In the mid-1970s the coal industry in the North East of England supported a fascinating web of rail freight operations, with numerous collieries, coking plants, power stations, export terminals and domestic coal depots still in operation. Only a small proportion of the region's coal traffic appeared in the working timetable because most flows covered only short distances and operated under local tripping arrangements; among the exceptions were trainload flows of containerised coke from Derwenthaugh to Wakefield and coking coal from Betteshanger to South Bank (Teesside).

The list of rail-connected coal locations in the North East in 1978, excluding domestic coal depots, was, north to south:

South Shilbottle	colliery
Widdrington	opencast disposal point
Butterwell	opencast disposal point
Ellington	colliery
Lynemouth	colliery
Ashington	colliery
Blyth Cambois	power station
Blyth West	export staithes
Blyth Bates	colliery
Blyth Bates	export staithes
Brenkley	colliery
Weetslade	colliery and washery
Backworth Eccles	colliery
Stella North	power station
Stella South	power station
Derwenthaugh	coking plant and washery
Clockburn	colliery
Swalwell	opencast disposal point
Dunston	export staithes
Dunston	power station
Norwood	coking plant

No 37032 takes the flyover line to gain access to Tyne Yard reception sidings with an unfitted coal train on 28 August 1974. Large numbers of HTO and HTV hoppers were refurbished and re-bodied in the 1970s, with five instead of two vertical reinforcing supports on each side, but in this train only the sixth wagon appears to have been re-bodied.
Tom Heavyside

Monkton	coking plant and washery
Jarrow	export staithes
Harton	export staithes
Westoe	colliery
Boldon	colliery
Herrington	colliery
Lambton	coking plant
Consett	BSC coke ovens
Wearmouth	colliery
Sunderland South Dock	export staithes
Dawdon	colliery
Seaham	export staithes
Seaham	colliery
Hawthorn	coking plant
South Hetton	colliery
Easington	colliery
Horden	colliery
East Hetton	colliery
Fishburn	coking plant
North Tees	power station
South Bank	BSC coke ovens
Lackenby	steelworks
Redcar	BSC coke ovens

Two distinctive features of rail-borne coal operations in the North East were staithes and rope-worked inclines. The staithes, located along the Tyne estuary and on the coast, were high-level sidings supported on a wooden framework, from which coal was discharged from hopper wagons via chutes into waiting ships.

The rope-worked inclines provided a convenient way of overcoming hilly terrain south of Newcastle without the need for expensive tunnels, viaducts and earthworks. One of the best-known rope-worked lines was the Bowes Railway, which originally stretched for 15 miles from Dipton to Dunston, its origins going back to 1727. The central section of the Bowes Railway, serving Kibblesworth colliery, closed in 1974.

By the end of the 1970s staithes were in decline throughout the region and rope-worked inclines were almost extinct. The last operational incline in the North East was from Hawthorn to Seaham, retained by the NCB to carry stone waste until the 1984/85 strike.

Bucking the trend of colliery cutbacks was the opening of Butterwell opencast disposal point in 1977, involving the re-opening of a former mineral line north of Ashington and the building of a new connection between Butterwell and the East Coast Main Line. Trains normally reached Butterwell from the Ashington direction but

Bagnall 0-6-0ST 'Austerity' No 2779 awaits its next duty at Vane Tempest colliery, Seaham, on 28 August 1974, as No 37045 departs with a trainload of unfitted hopper wagons. *Tom Heavyside*

Above The coal staithes at Sunderland South Dock were still in use in 1985, receiving deliveries in HTV hopper wagons. No 37024 departs with empties for Seaham Polka sidings on 22 July.

Below In 1982 BR carried a spot load of Polish coal from Lackenby to Hartlepool. No 31263 heads east at South Bank with empty HTO wagons returning from Hartlepool on 20 March.

departed via the East Coast Main Line, thereby avoiding a run-round movement.

While many North East coal flows in the 1970s still relied on elderly vacuum-braked or unfitted wagons, BR introduced air-braked HBA hoppers on coal traffic to Blyth Cambois 'A' and 'B' power stations. The HBAs later gave way to mgr stock, although the full economies of mgr operation could not be achieved because the track layout did not include a return loop.

After the miners' strike, coal traffic in the North East declined sharply. Some destinations, including Stella North and South power stations and Blyth Bates staithes, stopped receiving coal by rail. The collieries at Blyth Bates, Brenkley, Herrington, Horden and Ashington all closed between 1985 and 1988. The coking plants at Derwenthaugh, Lambton and Monkton were all deleted from the rail freight map in the mid-1980s, traffic from the Fishburn and Norwood plants having already ceased.

However, as in other parts of the country,

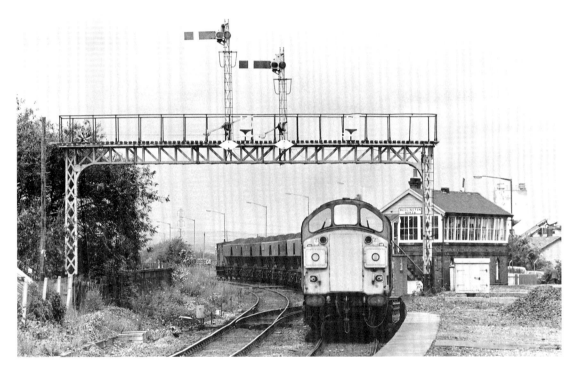

Above No 37066 rolls into Bedlington station on 21 June 1982 with 15 loaded HBA hoppers. Trains from the Northumberland opencast sites to Blyth had to run round here.

Below No 56080 is pictured just after arrival at Butterwell opencast disposal point with mgr wagons on 17 July 1986. It will later form a service to Blyth Cambois power station.

A classic colliery scene at Horden on the Durham coast, as No 37226 is about to depart with the 9H18 service to South Bank on 3 June 1982. The brake-van on the left will be attached to the rear of the train. Horden colliery was once the largest coal mine in Britain, reaching out to huge reserves under the sea; however, it suffered from flooding in later years and closed in 1987.

opencasting continued to thrive, using railheads at Widdrington, Butterwell and Swalwell. To clean up the environs of the Gateshead Metro Centre, the Swalwell opencast operation – which also handled deep-mined coal from non-rail-connected pits in County Durham – was transferred to a new rapid loading bunker at Wardley, opened in 1989 on the site of the long-closed Follingsby colliery.

At surviving collieries efforts were made to reduce operating costs by simplifying the loading arrangements and cutting out shunting and the use of industrial locomotives wherever possible. A new rapid loading bunker was provided at Dawdon

No 56117 pulls away from Wardley opencast disposal point with the 1125 departure to Cambois power station on 24 February 1995. To the right of the train are the disused tracks of the Leamside line, the subject of a re-opening proposal that was looking increasingly unlikely as this book went to press.

in 1986, replacing the complex track layout at the pithead. However, the adjacent sidings serving Seaham Harbour continued to receive trainloads of spoil from local collieries, such as Hawthorn, for dumping on the coastline.

An extraordinary survival on South Tyneside was the NCB electric railway linking Westoe colliery with Harton staithes. A remnant of the former South Shields, Marsden and Whitburn colliery railway, the line was operated on the 1,500 volt DC system and worked by a small stud of centre-cab locomotives. The railway carried both coal for export and shale for dumping at sea, using a sizeable fleet of NCB-owned loose-coupled hopper wagons. The coal traffic ceased in 1988 following the provision of new trackwork allowing BR trains direct access to Westoe colliery. The remaining shale trains, and the unique electric railway, were ousted by a new conveyor belt in the following year.

The closure of Ashington colliery heralded the end of another unusual industrial system, linking Ashington with Lynemouth, in December 1986. The system had used a sizeable fleet of ex-BR Class 14 diesels, acquired by the NCB after their premature withdrawal from main-line use in the late 1960s. Wooden-bodied wagons remained in use until the end. The traffic included coal from Lynemouth to Ashington for stocking and spoil from Ashington for dumping on the coast. The NCB also controlled the line between Ashington and Butterwell, although it was used only by BR trains.

The fate of the remaining coal staithes in the North East was sealed when much of their business was diverted to the new Tyne Coal Terminal in 1985. Constructed at a cost of £12 million, the Tyne Coal Terminal comprised a single discharge hopper capable of handling up to 21 trains a day. The importance of that terminal to the region, still reeling from the loss of traditional heavy industries, was marked by the presence of the Queen Mother at its opening. The project included a new west-facing curve on the Newcastle-Sunderland line so that coal trains could arrive directly from the Durham coast as well as from Northumberland and the Tyne Valley. The coal was shipped mainly to Thames estuary power stations at West Thurrock, Tilbury and Kingsnorth; however, a significant volume was also exported to the Scandinavian countries.

As well as allowing the run-down and closure of traditional staithes, the opening of the Tyne Coal Terminal hastened the modernisation of the region's coal wagon fleet. Many flows in the region, including those to the staithes, had been operated by vacuum-braked and unfitted hopper wagons, which were fast becoming life-expired and had no place in the soon to be privatised rail freight industry.

The last surviving rail-connected staithes were those at Blyth West. Dating back to 1928, they were 1,600 feet long and could berth two ships simultaneously. Although the tracks were originally designed for operation by gravity, the

Ashington colliery remained a hive of activity in the mid-1980s, with ex-BR Class 14 locomotives ferrying coal and shale over the NCB lines and Class 37s picking up coal trains for the short journey to Blyth. NCB No 31, formerly BR Class 14 No 9531, arrives at Ashington with a typically mixed rake of NCB wagons from Lynemouth on 17 July 1986.

facility was modernised to take the weight of a Class 08 shunter, and towards the end of its life it was able to receive merry-go-round hopper wagons, albeit still with manual discharge. The last shipments from Blyth West took place in December 1989.

A new destination for coal in 1986 was the ICI chemical plant at Wilton, on Teesside. Two of the plant's boilers were converted from oil to coal, and a rapid discharge facility was provided with the help of a Government Section 8 grant. In the early years BR operated one or two trains daily from Butterwell. By this time the previous flows of coal to BSC coking plants on Teesside had ceased.

●

BR's coal business benefited in the early 1990s from the opening of a second rapid discharge export terminal, at Blyth Bates. Located on the south side of the Blyth estuary on the site of Blyth Bates colliery, the terminal was built with the support of a £¼ million Section 8 grant and completed in 1991. The work included reconstructing the 2½-mile branch line from Newsham Junction, last used in 1984, together with new signalling and level crossing control. The new terminal handled a similar range of business to the Tyne Coal Terminal but was more conveniently situated for traffic from Northumberland. It also provided a useful back-up in case of problems at the Tyne Coal Terminal.

The buoyant volumes of opencast traffic were boosted in 1991 by the opening of Plenmeller opencast disposal point, just east of Haltwhistle on the Newcastle to Carlisle line. Initially the loaded trains from Plenmeller had to run via Carlisle, but extra trackwork was installed in 1993 so that trains could depart in an easterly direction and reach their destination – usually the Tyne Coal Terminal or Blyth Bates – more quickly. Plenmeller also dispatched some coal trains to Hope cement works.

The region's deep mines, meanwhile, continued to disappear. Dawdon and Murton closed in 1991, although stockpiled coal continued to be removed from Murton until 1993. The national pit closure programme of October 1992 spelt the end for all remaining North East pits except the highly productive Ellington complex – linked by conveyor to the Alcan power station at Lynemouth, but also the origin of trainloads of containerised domestic coal for the Irish market.

Some of the threatened pits were later reprieved. However, the reprieve was only temporary: Easington, Vane Tempest/Seaham and Westoe all wound their last coal in 1993, followed by Wearmouth – the last colliery in County Durham – in 1994. Stockpiled coal kept the sidings at Easington in use until 1995. Even Ellington pit stopped production in 1994, which led to the introduction of coal trains from Yorkshire to Lynemouth for the Alcan power station; however, the pit was subsequently re-opened by RJB Mining – later to become UK Coal – and managed to survive into the 21st century.

As for destinations, the shipment traffic through the Tyne Coal Terminal and Blyth Bates proved to be less regular than BR had hoped. In 1995 the Terminal was handling only four or five trains a day. The volume of coal delivered to Cambois power station was fluctuating too, although in 1995 Loadhaul won some useful long-distance traffic from Killoch to Cambois to complement flows from local loading points. Cambois later stopped receiving coal by rail and closed completely in 2000.

While coal flows to North East destinations declined, BR carried substantial tonnages of Durham and Northumberland coal to the Aire Valley power stations in the early 1990s, including some trains to Gascoigne Wood for 'sweetening' the output of the Selby coalfield. The points of origin included Hawthorn, Easington, Dawdon, Wardley, Butterwell and Widdrington.

Imported coal started to make an impression with the starting up of various flows from Redcar mineral terminal in the early 1990s. A short-term flow operated from Redcar to Longannet in 1992, but soon the emphasis was on southbound traffic, destined either for power stations such as Ferrybridge or for industrial locations including

To rebuild coal stocks after the miners' strike, BR ran a number of extra coal trains from Durham and Northumberland collieries to Aire Valley power stations. No 56007 passes the site of Hart station, north of Hartlepool, with 6G60, the 1405 York to South Dock empties, on Sunday 21 July 1985.

Cambois power station was still taking coal by rail in early 1995, with three or four deliveries on a typical day. On 21 February No 56091 departs from the power station sidings with the 1145 empties to Tyne Yard, while sister locomotive 56065 arrives with the 0846 service from Wardley.

In the summer of 1994 Loadhaul moved a large tonnage of coke from Redcar Mineral Terminal to British Steel Scunthorpe. No 56135 waits at Redcar while its rake of 35 HAAs is loaded on 24 August. In the 1990s Redcar became a busy loading point for imported coal to various power stations and cement works.

Ketton, Clitheroe, Penyffordd, Lostock and Winnington. Redcar replaced Butterwell as the supplier of coal to Wilton in 1996. Loadhaul also began operating trainloads of coke in HEA wagons from Redcar to Scunthorpe, a flow that continued into the EWS era and was joined in 2005 by containerised coke from Redcar to Port Talbot.

The reprieve of Ellington colliery limited the amount of coal that needed to be delivered by rail to Alcan at Lynemouth. However, Alcan installed a rapid discharge facility at its plant and trains ran from various locations in the mid-1990s including Hatfield, Wintersett and Redcar. In 2004 and 2005 EWS supplied Lynemouth with coal from Tyne Dock, while in 2005 its competitor Freightliner Heavy Haul ran services from Immingham. Meanwhile, despite substantial investment by UK Coal, Ellington colliery finally closed in February 2005 as a result of flooding problems, bringing an abrupt end to centuries of deep mining in the North East.

The use of the Tyne Coal Terminal and Blyth Bates for export traffic diminished as local coal sources dried up and as sea-fed customers turned to cheaper imports via Rotterdam. By the end of the 1990s the Terminal was exporting no coal at all, and Blyth Bates saw little use other than a short-term flow from Butterwell in 1998. The tracks to the Tyne Coal Terminal were kept shiny by other traffic flows, including cars, containers, scrap metal and imported coal, but the Blyth Bates branch fell into disuse after an all too short period of revival.

The opencast disposal points at Butterwell and Widdrington remained in use in 2005, but those at Plenmeller and Wardley had closed by the end of the 1990s. When EWS won a short-term contract to move opencast coal from the Team Valley, near Tyne Yard, in 2003, it had to search hard for a new loading point and eventually settled on the lime terminal at Thrislington, there being no other rail-served sites in the area with sufficient space for stockpiling and adequate road access.

The majority of coal trains in the North East in 2005 were simply passing through, using Tyne Yard as a staging point on their journey from Scottish opencast sites and Hunterston import terminal to power stations in the Aire and Trent Valleys. Within the region, the industry that once gave rise to the saying 'to carry coals to Newcastle' had virtually ceased to exist.

9.

Scotland

The coal-mining area in Scotland stretched from Ayrshire across the Central Belt to Lothian and Fife. In 1977 some 20 pits retained a rail connection, although many produced only small tonnages of coal. The NCB still used steam locomotives at a number of locations more than a decade after diesels had taken over on the main line. The last colliery to use steam on a regular basis in Scotland was Bedlay, in the Monklands district north of Coatbridge, persisting right up to the colliery's closure in December 1981.

While some of the coal from Scottish pits was destined for power stations, a major NCB customer in the Central Belt was Ravenscraig steelworks. However, in the late 1970s British Steel decided to switch to imported coal. The company built a massive loading terminal at Hunterston deep-water port, which would handle imports of both coal and iron ore. Industrial strife delayed the opening of the terminal, but from March 1980 frequent block trains operated between Hunterston and Ravenscraig, carrying either iron ore in 102-tonne tippler wagons or coal in standard merry-go-round hoppers.

British Steel was not the first merry-go-round customer in Scotland. The South of Scotland Electricity Board (SSEB) had set up rapid discharge terminals at its Longannet and Cockenzie power stations by the early 1970s. The layout at Longannet was particularly elaborate with a continuous loop and two triangular junctions allowing trains to arrive and depart either via Dunfermline or via Stirling. The power station was fully commissioned in 1973 and ranked as Britain's second biggest, with its installed capacity of 2,400MW; Cockenzie was built in 1968 with only 1,200MW capacity.

Older power stations such as Kincardine and Townhill had only basic rail facilities and continued to take coal in vacuum-braked or

This view of Kinneil colliery, Bo'ness, gives an idea of the complex loading and shunting arrangements found at many pitheads until the 1970s. Both loaded and empty wagons were often left for long periods in colliery sidings, which meant that BR had to maintain an artificially large wagon fleet. No 20099 is ready to pull its rake of 21-ton wagons away on 24 May 1974; the brake-van on the left will be attached to the rear of the train. Simmering in the shed is 0-4-0 saddle tank AB2292, still in regular use at that time. *Tom Heavyside*

One of the regular flows handled at Killoch was slurry for Methil power station. The slurry could not be carried in hopper wagons and BR continued to use vacuum-braked MSV wagons until 1990. Nos 37674 and 37675 wait while their train is loaded at Killoch on 6 April 1989.

One of the regular flows handled at Killoch was slurry for Methil power station. The slurry could not be carried in hopper wagons and BR continued to use vacuum-braked MSV wagons until 1990. Nos 37674 and 37675 wait while their train is loaded at Killoch on 6 April 1989.

unfitted wagons. No attempt was made to introduce merry-go-round stock to Methil power station, which opened 1965 and was designed to burn low-grade coal slurry from Westfield and other Scottish sources.

●

By the start of the 1984/85 miners' strike, only eight Scottish pits remained in operation: Barony, Polkemmet, Bilston Glen, Monktonhall, Seafield/Frances, Polmaise, Comrie and Longannet. No rail traffic operated out of Longannet because the pit was connected by a 5½-mile cable belt conveyor to Longannet power station. Opencast coal was beginning to make its mark in Scotland, with a rapid loading bunker established at Blindwells on the eastern fringe of the Lothian coalfield. BR carried much of the output from Blindwells to Cockenzie power station – a distance of about a mile as the crow flies! In Fife, opencast coal including slurry for Methil was loaded at Westfield, at the end of a 5-mile freight-only branch from Thornton yard.

Located beside the East Coast Main Line, Blindwells was one of the earliest opencast disposal points in Scotland, and sent much of its output to Cockenzie power station, a distance of about a mile as the crow flies. No 56108 prepares to depart from Blindwells with HBA wagons on 13 July 1992.

No 37262 *Dounreay* departs from Thornton with the 7G01 working from Methil power station to Westfield on 27 August 1990, comprising 28 MSV wagons for loading with slurry. The structures on the skyline, between the signals, belong to the ill-fated Rothes colliery, which flooded before its planned opening.

Class 25 No 5160 passes the long-closed Waterside station with a trainload of coal from Dunaskin washery to Ayr on 30 August 1973. The traffic from Dunaskin finished in 1986 but the line subsequently re-opened for opencast coal from Chalmerston. The former iron works on the left became the Dunaskin Open Air Museum. *Tom Heavyside*

The end of the strike left the mining industry north of the border in a perilous state, just as it did in England and Wales. A case in point was Polkemmet, which had once been the second biggest employer in West Lothian and one of the most successful mines in Scotland. It supplied good-quality coking coal with a low sulphur content, much of it destined for Ravenscraig until the late 1970s. Unfortunately the workings were damaged by flooding during the strike and the NCB could not justify the expense of recovery.

Other pit closures in the period 1986-88 were Comrie and the Seafield/Frances complex in Fife and Polmaise on the south side of Stirling. At Comrie, BR had served the Rexco coking plant as well as the colliery; both were reached by an NCB line from Oakley exchange sidings. The coastal pithead at Seafield was one of the most modern in Scotland, dating back only to 1960; its workings

were merged with neighbouring Frances colliery in the early 1980s.

In Ayrshire, coal loading at Barony colliery and at Dunaskin and Knockshinnoch washeries had ceased by the mid-1980s. But that decade also saw the beginnings of major growth in opencast extraction. A new rapid loader was installed at the former colliery site of Knockshinnoch in 1985, partly funded by a grant from the European Economic Community. Trains carried coal from Knockshinnoch to Ayr Harbour, where it was shipped to Northern Ireland for burning at Belfast West and Kilroot power stations. The investment included new Westinghouse door-closing equipment at Ayr Harbour so that the coal could be carried in merry-go-round wagons; previously it had been delivered in manual-discharge HBA hoppers. For the domestic market, BR carried two or three weekly trainloads from Knockshinnoch to Falkland yard for onward delivery by Speedlink to

Above No 27212 pulls away from Ayr Harbour with 15 empty HBA hoppers for Dunaskin washery on 25 August 1981. Although intended mainly for domestic coal, the HBAs spent many years on trainload flows to destinations without mgr discharge facilities.

Right Rapid loading facilities were provided at Knockshinnoch in 1985, mainly for traffic to Ayr Harbour, but by the late 1990s Knockshinnoch was supplying mainly the English and Scottish power generators. No 56045 draws forward under the rapid loader before working the 7Z39 departure to Carlisle on 16 July 1998.

the Roche Products plant at Dalry. A short-term contract also operated from Knockshinnoch to Fiddlers Ferry, foreshadowing much larger-scale movements on that route a decade later.

Further growth in Ayrshire opencast traffic took place in 1988/89. BR's Coal sub-sector met the £200,000 cost of re-opening the Annbank to Mauchline line, previously closed under the 1985 Ayrshire re-signalling scheme, in order to provide a shorter route from Knockshinnoch to Ayr Harbour. The new opencast disposal point at Chalmerston was connected to the rail network by re-opening the recently abandoned Waterside branch and building a 1½-mile extension on a former colliery railway alignment.

The opencast disposal point and washery at Killoch had its rail connection revived for four flows: inward coal from Chalmerston; outward

RAIL FREIGHT: COAL

Left Several rakes of MCV mineral wagons and HBA hoppers await discharge at Ayr Harbour on 25 August 1981, as an unidentified Class 08 locomotive shunts four more HBAs into position.

Below Ayr Harbour saw an upsurge in export coal traffic in the late 1980s and a new hopper discharge terminal was provided to shorten discharge times. Pilot loco 08727 stands at the seaward end of a rake of 16 HAAs on 4 April 1989, loaded with coal that had arrived the previous day from Knockshinnoch. The export traffic to Northern Ireland dwindled in the 1990s.

Left Passing the re-instated junction at Annbank on 13 July 1988 are Nos 20227 and 20192 with 6R04, the 1147 from Knockshinnoch to Ayr Harbour. The line from Mauchline to Annbank had only recently been re-opened, following the growth in traffic from Knockshinnoch.

The opening of Chalmerston coal loading point involved the re-laying of tracks on a long-abandoned mineral line. No 66216 runs round its train of HAA wagons after working 6R72, the 1435 from Falkland yard, on 27 August 2003.

coal to Ayr Harbour for export to Ireland; outward slurry to Methil; and outward coal for Haymarket. Outside Ayrshire a new opencast loading terminal was provided at Ravenstruther, near Carstairs, to carry coal from the Douglas Basin to Ayr Harbour. The upsurge in rail traffic to Ayr Harbour – the target figure in 1990 was 1¼ million tonnes – justified the building of a new hopper discharge pit and elevator at the port, capable of handling 1,000 tonnes of coal per hour.

On the eastern side of the coalfield the shift from deep-mined to surface extraction saw the opening of a new opencast disposal point at Roughcastle, near Falkirk, in 1986, while the deep mine at Bilston Glen, reached by a 5-mile branch south of Millerhill, closed in 1989.

BR continued to move large quantities of imported coal from Hunterston to Ravenscraig, amounting to four daily 46-wagon trainloads in the summer of 1988. A short-term flow ran from Hunterston to Longannet in 1988/89, challenging the near monopoly of British Coal in supplying Scotland's largest power station. Another point of entry for imported coal was Rothesay Dock, on the north side of the Clyde, where the rail connection was temporarily re-activated in 1988 for traffic to SSEB power stations. Trains ran initially to Kincardine – the first deliveries by rail to that location for a number of years – and later to Longannet and Cockenzie. A further short-term flow in 1990 was imported coke from Hunterston Low Level to Scunthorpe, using HEA hopper wagons.

●

In the early 1990s the closure of Ravenscraig steelworks dealt a huge blow to rail freight in Scotland, depriving BR of some of its highest-volume and most lucrative flows north of the border. Among the casualties were the coal movements from Hunterston to Ravenscraig,

The intensive coal flow from Hunterston to British Steel Ravenscraig used rakes of 46 HAAs hauled by a pair of Class 37s; a third locomotive was attached for the final climb from Mossend to Ravenscraig. Nos 37310 *British Steel Ravenscraig* and 37311 *British Steel Hunterston* could scarcely be more appropriate traction for 7D09, the 1025 departure from Hunterston, pictured near Dubbs Junction on 5 April 1989.

The Rothesay Dock branch was revived in 1988 for a short-term flow of imported coal to SSEB power stations. Nos 26004 and 26007 propel empty HEA wagons into the loading area at Rothesay Dock on 12 July 1988, having arrived with 6Z63, the 1005 departure from Kincardine.

which had only recently benefited from the introduction of Class 60 haulage. Another Scottish coal loss was the mothballing of Knockshinnoch opencast disposal point in 1992; however, the other opencast sites remained active and Blindwells gained a short-term flow of containerised coal to Bennerley in the East Midlands in 1993. The slurry traffic to Methil was finally converted to air-braked operation, using railway-owned open box wagons.

In the brief Transrail era, opencast developments included new loading points at Grangemouth and Thornton and, in December 1996, the re-opening of Knockshinnoch. The main destinations for Scottish coal were still Longannet, Cockenzie and Ayr Harbour, but the traffic from Grangemouth included regular trains to Fiddlers Ferry in North West England. Meanwhile Scottish Power invested in clean-burn technology at both Longannet and Cockenzie, extending their life considerably. However, Scottish Power's plans to build a new £120m coal-fired power station at Kincardine did not come to fruition.

The former British Steel import terminal at Hunterston, disused since 1993, was a valuable facility just waiting to be taken over by a new operator. It duly re-opened under Clydeport management in 1997 for flows of imported coal to Eastern Group power stations at Drakelow,

High Marnham and West Burton. By 1998 Hunterston was dispatching up to 11 trainloads of coal a day, destined for both Scottish and English power generators. The English traffic stretched the capacity of the former Glasgow & South Western line via Dumfries, some of which had been reduced to single track as an economy measure.

Monktonhall colliery dispatched its last trainload of coal in 1997, having operated as a miners' co-operative since 1992. That closure left Longannet as the last deep mine in Scotland, still linked by conveyor to the adjacent power station. Opencast movements fluctuated as reserves became available or exhausted and as contracts were won and lost with the power generators. The losses in 1999/2000 included coal from Blindwells and slurry from Westfield; rail traffic to Methil ceased as Scottish Power relegated the station to part of its strategic reserve.

However, the low sulphur content of Scottish coal and the high demand from Scottish Power helped to promote a number of new opencast sites and loading points. In Fife the former power station sidings at Kincardine came back into use in 1997 as a loading point for coal from various sites on the north side of the Forth estuary, such as Forest Mill. The coal was then conveyed by rail to Longannet; bizarrely, the road leg of the journey was longer than the rail leg, but the reason for

Sample programme for Ayrshire coal, January 1997									
	Number of booked trains								
Origin	Su	M	T	W	Th	F	S	Destination	Wagons
Hunterston	-	2	2	2	2	2	2	Longannet	HAA
Hunterston	-	1	2	2	2	2	-	High Marnham	HAA
Chalmerston	-	2	2	2	2	2	-	Killoch	HAA
Killoch	-	1	2	1	1	1	-	Ayr Harbour	HAA
Killoch	-	1	1	1	1	1	-	Longannet	HAA
Killoch	-	1	1	1	1	1	-	Methil	SSA
Killoch	-	-	-	-	-	-	-	Blackburn	HEA
Knockshinnoch	-	3	3	3	3	3	2	Longannet	HAA
Knockshinnoch	-	-	1	-	1	-	-	Ayr Harbour	HAA
Ayr Harbour	-	-	-	-	1	-	-	Fiddlers Ferry	HAA

The former British Steel deep-water port and rapid loading facility at Hunterston gained a new lease of life in 1997 when it started forwarding imported coal for the power generators. No 60038 arrives at Hunterston with hooded HFA wagons in torrential rain on 12 February 1997. It will later form the 1155 departure to Drakelow.

using rail was to overcome the restriction on lorry movements through the village of Kincardine. EWS provided a cost-effective service from Kincardine simply by extending the journey of trains on the existing Longannet circuit; a train from Westfield, for example, discharged its load as usual at Longannet, but then formed a working to Kincardine and back before returning empty to Westfield or Thornton yard. Another new opencast loading point in Fife was Inverkeithing.

In the Central Belt, a coal loading point was established in the down sidings at Mossend yard, while a more ambitious scheme saw the re-opening of about a mile of the former Coltness branch in 2000 to serve an opencast site at Watsonhead, with a life expectancy of three years. In the Lothian district opencast loading took place at Millerhill yard; however, the main function of Millerhill was to stage the increasing number of trains carrying Scottish coal to power stations in the Aire and Trent Valleys.

Ayrshire opencast operations continued to expand from the late 1990s onwards. A short stretch of the former Holehouse Junction to Rankinston line, closed in 1950, re-opened in 1998 for a short-term flow from Broomhill. No run-round facilities were provided and trains had to be propelled from Holehouse Junction to

The opencast site at Westfield was once the biggest of its kind in Scotland. No 37262 departs with 6G01 to Thornton on 28 August 1990, carrying coal for the Aire Valley. The weight restriction over the Forth Bridge made this a complex journey: two trains of 36 wagons had to be re-formed into three trains of 24 wagons for the Thornton-Millerhill leg.

Broomhill with a brake-van leading the formation.

In 1999 a £2.5 million Freight Facilities Grant was awarded to Law Mining for a new opencast loading point at New Cumnock, expected to produce 1.7 million tonnes of coal over a five-year period. The first train ran in September 2000; the destinations served included Rugeley, Drakelow, Ratcliffe, Cottam, Drax, Lynemouth and Hope.

Two further line re-openings were authorised in 2002/03 to cater for new opencast flows. The first was the proposed re-instatement of part of the Auchinleck-Muirkirk branch, closed to passengers in 1950, to serve a new Scottish Coal opencast site at Powharnal. The Scottish Executive awarded a £9.75 million FFG towards the Powharnal project in February 2002, although it took another seven months before the mine itself received planning permission, and in 2005 the project was understood to be subject to further delay.

The second proposal involved relaying 2 miles of a long-abandoned mineral branch from North Boig (on the Knockshinnoch branch) to a new site at Greenburn, operated by Kier Mining. The Scottish Executive announced a £3.9 million FFG for that scheme in August 2003 and the first train ran in May 2004. Trains ran from Greenburn to Cockenzie, Ironbridge and Drax, all routed via Falkland yard for operational reasons.

In addition, opencast traffic from Chalmerston, Killoch and Knockshinnoch continued into the 21st century. However, the traffic pattern was very different from that established in the 1980s, with exports through Ayr Harbour having dwindled and no inward traffic to Killoch. Instead, trains ran direct from Chalmerston, Killoch and Knockshinnoch to English and Scottish power stations, with individual flows changing week by week.

The capacity of the former Glasgow & South Western line was improved by the provision of a southbound loop at Thornhill, although the number of paths was still restricted by the single-track bottleneck between Annan and Gretna Junction and by long block sections elsewhere. In 2005 the G&SW line was carrying up to 20 loaded coal trains a day from Hunterston and the opencast loading points – far more than BR planners could have imagined when the line was rationalised.

The closure of Longannet colliery after severe flooding in 2002 meant that more coal for Longannet power station would require transportation. The use of rail was not a foregone conclusion – delivery by barge from Rosyth was also considered – but in 2003 Scottish Power opted for a seven-year contract with Clydeport for up to 5 million tonnes a year from Hunterston. That contract started in May 2004, with EWS moving 12 30-wagon merry-go-round trains each weekday – and on Saturdays – from Hunterston to Longannet. A small amount of coal also continued to be delivered from Thornton, although that had ceased by 2005.

The economics of the Hunterston-Longannet

Problems at Longannet colliery brought increased rail traffic to Longannet power station in 1997 – a taste of things to come, as the colliery would soon be closed. Mainline Freight-liveried Class 60 No 60088 *Buachaille Etive Mor* skirts the Firth of Forth at Culross with empties from Longannet on 14 February 1997.

flow were improved by increasing the permitted train length to 38 wagons. However, the Forth Bridge was not able to accept EWS's new bogie HTA hoppers, which were taking over many power station flows in other parts of the country. For a solution to that issue, EWS would have to wait for the re-opening of the 13-mile Stirling-Alloa-Kincardine line, closed as a through route since 1981.

The long-awaited Alloa line revival came a step closer when the Scottish Parliament agreed to provide 81% of the capital costs of the project. The green light for construction was given in August 2005, with an expected completion date of summer 2007. EWS had argued that the re-opening would not only benefit its own operation, by reducing the journey time and increasing the tonnage per train between Hunterston and Longannet, but would also allow the re-allocation of some existing freight paths over the Forth Bridge for an expanded passenger service.

However, the potential sting in the tail for EWS was that the new route would also be usable by Freightliner Heavy Haul and any other companies wishing to enter the market.

The port of Leith became a loading point for imported coal in 2005, with two sidings re-instated to handle coal bound for Cockenzie. Between May and December 2005 EWS moved more than 500,000 tonnes of coal on that route. As with a number of import locations, Leith had previously been an export location for Scottish coal.

Opencast developments in Fife in 2004 included the re-opening (again!) of the Westfield branch, for flows to power stations such as Cockenzie, Ironbridge, Ratcliffe and Cottam. Loading at Kincardine had ceased, but EWS was now moving up to four trains a day from Thornton, mainly for the English power generators, and typically one daily train from Inverkeithing. A possible new loading point on the Methil branch was also under discussion.

With plenty more 'black gold' waiting to be claimed from the Scottish landscape, and with the announcement in February 2006 that Longannet power station will have flue gas desulphurisation equipment fitted to extend its life beyond 2015, Britain's rail freight operators north of the border are looking forward to a busy future.

10.

Wagonload coal

There was a time when almost every station in the country had a goods yard, receiving wagonloads of coal along with other everyday commodities for use in homes, offices, schools and factories. The growth of road transport after the Second World War began to erode the railway's traditional business, but until the early 1960s the network of station coal sidings and pick-up goods trains serving them remained largely intact.

The Beeching report of 1961 highlighted wagonload coal as one of the areas needing urgent rationalisation. At that time 61% of the total coal moved by British Railways was transported by the wagonload, amounting to some 28.1 million tons. That traffic was theoretically spread between 5,031 stations; however, in reality 1,172 of the stations had received no coal in the previous 12 months and a further 1,790 had received less than six wagons a week. At the other end of the scale, the busiest 1% of the stations received 20% of the total wagonload coal tonnage between them.

Given that British Railways was unable to make its smaller-scale customers pay a high enough charge to cover its costs, Beeching came to the conclusion that is now accepted as axiomatic: the railway must concentrate on what it does best, namely moving freight in large quantities or over long distances – and preferably both. Beeching proposed the closure of most station coal yards and their replacement by a few hundred coal concentration depots, where the high throughput would justify investment in mechanised handling and special-purpose road vehicles.

Like many good ideas in railway history, the proposal for strategically located coal concentration depots was implemented in part.

Many examples were established in London and the South East, such as the West Drayton depot, which became the busiest of its kind in the country. But in some areas BR and its customers were slow to invest in new facilities. Although by the mid-1970s the cull of small goods depots in rural areas was largely complete, the total number of locations open for coal traffic was still greater than Beeching had proposed. Even the new coal concentration depots rarely received trainload deliveries from a single colliery; they were usually served by wagonload trip workings from the local marshalling yard.

One area where small coal yards survived a long time was North East England. The following stations and private sidings, many of them raised coal 'drops' modelled on North Eastern Railway practice, were still open for wagonload coal in 1978:

Alnmouth • Birtley • Blackhill • Blaydon • Brotton • Carlin How • Consett • Darlington Hopetown • Dunston • Durham • Ferryhill • Gateshead Park Lane • Haltwhistle • Hartlepool Cliff House • Hartlepool Throston Bridge • Heaton • Hexham • Jarrow • Lambton • Middlesbrough Lloyd Street • Middlesbrough Richmond Street • Middlesbrough Vulcan Street • Morpeth • Newcastle Railway Street • Newcastle Victoria Yard • North Shields • Redcar Central • Saltburn • Shildon • South Bank • Stockton Millfield • Stockton South • Sunderland Deptford • Sunderland Millfield • Sunderland South Dock • Tweedmouth • Tyne Dock Victoria Road • Tyne Dock West End • Tynemouth

Above The legend 'House coal concentration' is visible on the sides of this uniform rake of hopper wagons, heading east through Sonning cutting in June 1970. The traction is an unidentified 'Warship' diesel-hydraulic, nearing the end of its short life following BR's decision to standardise on diesel-electric types. *J. H. Cooper-Smith*

Below Different grades of coal from Dunaskin washery are evident in this view of No 27010 near Waterside, on the former Dalmellington branch, on 21 May 1974. At that time the Class 27s were commonplace on Scottish freight and passenger workings; the class became extinct on BR in 1987. *Tom Heavyside*

Below Scotland's most northerly station: two mineral wagons await unloading at Thurso on 24 September 1980, as No 26042 stands ready to form the next passenger departure to Inverness. At that time the Far North line still had a daily pick-up freight service and coal was handled at several intermediate stations as well as Thurso. After 1984 the coal traffic in the Highlands was concentrated on Inverness, although for a short period in the late 1990s Thurso received coal again in containers.

During the 1970s wagonload coal traffic continued to decline, as more and more householders replaced coal fires with central heating and as road transport became more efficient. Many of the surviving traditional coal yards closed and some coal concentration depots became prematurely redundant too. A case in point was Wolverton coal concentration depot, which opened in 1966 but was converted to a roadstone terminal for the new town of Milton Keynes as early as 1972. Conversely, two unlikely survivors were the small station coal yards at Guiseley and Menston on the Ilkley branch, both still open in 1981.

The network of coal loading points also continued to contract, mainly as a direct consequence of colliery closures. However, not all coal traffic came from collieries; there was substantial business from various coking plants and patent fuel works, including Phurnacite at Abercwmboi, Homefire at Coventry, Rexco at Ollerton and Comrie, and Coalite at Bolsover and Grimethorpe.

●

BR's attempts to streamline its wagonload operations led to the setting up of the air-braked Speedlink network. However, despite the introduction of a fleet of air-braked domestic coal hoppers, originally coded HBA, coal was one of the last traffic types to be transferred to Speedlink. The HBA wagons meanwhile found themselves deployed mainly on trainload flows, with significant numbers concentrated in Ayrshire, Northumberland and the East Midlands.

In May 1983 BR closed its traditional wagonload network to most types of freight, but some coal and scrap metal flows continued to run in vacuum-braked wagons until May 1984. During those 12 months the network of coal depots was heavily rationalised (see Appendix 1), either because the customer was unwilling to invest in equipment suitable for the new rolling-stock or because the traffic volume had become too low to sustain a regular service. The transition period brought the complication of trip workings

The once extensive network of freight lines at Barrow-in-Furness had been reduced to just a handful of sidings by the early 1980s, but there were still two separate coal depots – Cart and Hackett. No 25221 deposits four loaded mineral wagons at Hackett depot on 14 July 1983, before taking the rest of its train further down the branch to Cart sidings. A complex sequence of manoeuvres was necessary to exchange loaded for empty wagons at the two depots; on this occasion spirited working ensured that the job was complete within half an hour.

Four HTO coal hoppers roll into the down sidings at Tees Yard on 25 May 1982, while yard pilot No 08085 waits to return to the reception sidings for another rake of wagons. Soon scenes like this would pass into history, with the withdrawal of BR's remaining vacuum-braked coal hoppers and the end of hump shunting at Tees.

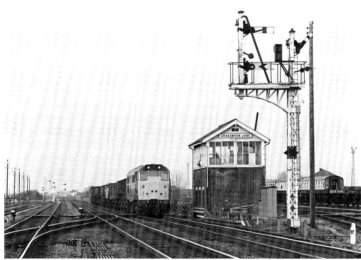

The 'Joint Line' from Lincoln to March via Sleaford and Spalding enabled freight from Nottinghamshire to East Anglia to avoid using the East Coast Main Line. No 31227 passes Grassmoor Junction on the approach to Whitemoor yard with the 7P04 from Mansfield Concentration Sidings on 13 January 1981, conveying coal for St Neots, Cambridge, Colchester Hythe and Broxbourne. The 'Joint Line' between Spalding and Whitemoor was closed in November 1982, but Whitemoor yard lasted into the 1990s as a Speedlink marshalling point.

Still conveyed in vacuum-braked hopper wagons, coal for Hove concentration depot is hauled through Shoreham-by-Sea on 26 August 1983. The train is the 1243 from Fratton to Brighton Top Yard, hauled by No 73121. Hove depot survived into the Speedlink Coal era but was then served from Redhill instead of via Fratton.

Above No 46049 passes Bensham with the 6C30 Speedlink service from Tyneside Central Freight Depot to Dagenham Dock on 10 May 1982. The eight HEA wagons are carrying coke from Derwenthaugh to Dagenham. Most wagonload coal traffic at that time was still conveyed in vacuum-braked wagons.

Below The Roche Products plant at Dalry received coal from Knockshinnoch in the late 1980s, and the wagons were tripped between Falkland yard and Dalry on the daily Speedlink service. Empty HAAs are included in the consist of 6R02, returning from Dalry to Falkland, on 4 April 1989. The motive power is No 26041, in old Railfreight livery with Eastfield depot's 'Scottie dog' emblem.

One of the first coal concentration depots to handle air-braked wagons was Aylesbury, although at first the new stock was conveyed by the normal wagonload network and trains often had to run partially fitted (ie with the automatic brake inoperative on either vacuum- or air-braked vehicles) with a brake-van at the rear. No 25032 pauses at Princes Risborough after arriving with the 8T16 trip working from Aylesbury on 7 April 1983. Here the wagons will be attached to a vacuum-braked service to Acton yard. Coal traffic to Aylesbury ceased in 1988 but the terminal remained open for roadstone from the Midlands.

conveying both air-braked and vacuum-braked wagons; this often meant coupling the air-braked wagons next to the locomotive and operating the vacuum-braked coal wagons in unfitted mode with a brake-van at the rear.

BR soon realised that the national Speedlink network was not ideally suited to domestic coal traffic. The main Speedlink hubs such as Willesden, Bescot, Warrington and Mossend bore little relation to the needs of coal distribution and some flows had to follow a circuitous route from colliery to coal depot. The miners' strike of 1984/85 brought a reduction in overall traffic volume – BR carried only 1.35 million tonnes of domestic coal in 1985/86 compared with a planned volume of 2 million tonnes – which

worsened the economics of an already marginal operation.

The solution was to set up a separate wagonload network for coal, with hubs located mainly in coal-producing areas. Not only would many flows cover a shorter distance, thereby reducing costs, but also the new network would enable the sharing of infrastructure, traction and traincrew resources with trainload coal operations, rather than with the general freight business with its very different geographical spread. Early BR documents used the term 'discrete coal network' for the new services, but the title 'Speedlink Coal' was soon adopted instead.

An example of improved efficiency was the servicing of Preston Deepdale coal depot. Coal from West Yorkshire to Deepdale had previously been sent by a Speedlink trip working from the colliery to Healey Mills, then by a Speedlink trunk service to Warrington, and finally by a trip working to Deepdale. Under the new system BR would run a dedicated coal train direct from Healey Mills to Deepdale, covering a much shorter route via Hebden Bridge and Blackburn.

The implementation of Speedlink Coal took place in four stages: November 1986, January 1987, March 1987 and July 1987. Once the final stage was in place, trunk services operated

RAIL FREIGHT: COAL

Above At dusk on 27 February 1981, electro-diesel No 73125 departs from Acton yard with the 6O81 feeder service to Wimbledon, consisting entirely of HTV hopper wagons. The marshalling of wagonload traffic at Acton yard ceased in 1984, with Willesden becoming the main hub for Speedlink services in the London area.

Below A short stretch of the former Longridge branch remained in use to serve Preston Deepdale coal concentration depot. In later years the line was subject to a 20mph speed limit and fly-tipping became an increasing problem. No 56075 nears its destination with the 0557 Healey Mills to Deepdale Speedlink Coal service on 4 August 1989, conveying Phurnacite from Abercwmboi.

Didcot was chosen as a Speedlink Coal yard because of the potential synergy with Trainload Coal traffic to Didcot power station. Feeder services operated from Didcot to all Southern Region coal depots and to Aylesbury, Neasden, West Drayton, Bow (via Temple Mills), Padworth and Westbury. No 37220 leaves Didcot with 6O86, the 1819 departure to either Fratton or Totton, on 31 July 1987.

between Millerhill, Healey Mills, Toton, Washwood Heath, Didcot, Radyr and Pantyffynnon yards. Most sections of the core network had two trains a day in each direction; those trains linking two coal-producing regions often carried both loaded and empty wagons in the same direction. The selection of Didcot as a marshalling point was designed to allow the sharing of traincrew resources with mgr trains to Didcot power station.

Feeder services linked the yards with 28 collieries and patent fuel plants, 37 coal concentration depots and two industrial private sidings. Most of the feeder services ran once a day, but some trains ran to different terminals on different days of the week in order to achieve higher loadings and make more effective use of resources. Depots on the Central and South Eastern divisions of the Southern Region, for example, were served as in the table below.

Fourteen additional coal depots, mainly in outlying locations, continued to be served by normal Speedlink services; these were Inverness, Elgin, Keith, Aberdeen, Dundee, Thornton, Carlisle, Birkenhead, Llandudno Junction, Small Heath, Grimsby, Lincoln, Lowestoft and Drinnick Mill. Conversely, a few of the new Speedlink Coal services carried non-coal traffic, such as cement to Preston Deepdale and wine tankers to Aylesbury.

The Speedlink Coal network was complemented by two through trains from Grimethorpe to Mossend, running on Sundays only and conveying smokeless fuel for distribution by road throughout Scotland. To serve the Northern Irish market BR ran dedicated trunk trains from South Wales and Lynemouth to Ellesmere Port, using 20-foot Cawoods containers on PFA wagons.

An important benefit of Speedlink Coal was that it made dedicated bottom-line management possible in an organisation that was now shaped by business sectors and sub-sectors. Most Speedlink Coal services were to be hauled by a fleet of 25 Class 37 locomotives based at Cardiff Canton,

MX	6O41	0118 Didcot-Plumstead	arr 0310	loaded to Plumstead, Hove and Purley, loaded to Ashford (WSO)
MX	6Y34	0410 Plumstead-Hove	arr 0620	empties from Plumstead, loaded to Hove and Purley, loaded to Ashford (WSO)
SX	6H23	1030 Hove-Redhill	arr 1133	empties from Plumstead and Hove, loaded to Purley, loaded to Ashford (MWO)
SX	6H23	1154 Redhill-Purley	arr 1208	loaded to Purley, loaded to Ashford (MWO)
MWO	6A51	1315 Purley-Ashford	arr 1530	empties from Purley, loaded to Ashford
MWO	6Y79	1615 Ashford-Redhill	arr 1858	empties from Purley and Ashford
MWSX	6A51	1315 Purley-Redhill	arr 1335	empties from Purley
SX	6V04	2130 Redhill-Didcot	arr 2343	empties from Purley, Plumstead and Hove, empties from Ashford (MWO)

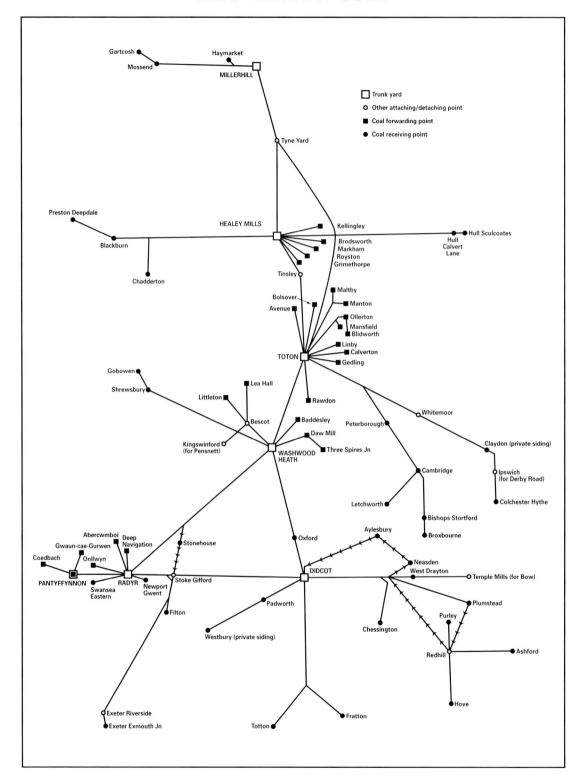

The Speedlink Coal network, July 1987.

The Chessington branch retained two coal concentration depots in the Speedlink Coal era: Tolworth and Chessington South. No 37197 positions three loaded HEAs at Chessington South after arriving with 6O66, the 1020 departure from Didcot, on 29 October 1987.

The last revenue-earning duty for a Class 03 shunter on BR was at Birkenhead, where some of the dockside lines were unable to take heavier locomotives. No 03073 takes empty HEAs from Birkenhead North coal depot to Cavendish sidings on 13 February 1989, where main-line traction will take over. The use of Class 03s at Birkenhead ceased in the following month.

Pilot loco 08692 propels a single HEA hopper towards the weighbridge at Small Heath coal depot on 22 May 1987. Small Heath did not generate enough traffic for a Speedlink Coal service and received deliveries by the normal Speedlink network until its closure in 1990.

with a single Class 33 allocated to internal Southern Region workings. The wagons were mainly 60mph HEA hoppers, a re-sprung version of the 45mph HBA type. However, the depots at West Drayton, Gartcosh and Inverness received some or all of their coal in 30-foot containers on FPA wagons.

BR's insistence on using either hopper wagons or containers meant that it could only serve suitably equipped terminals. The provision of a hopper discharge pit and conveyor, or container lifting equipment, did not come cheaply. An inexpensive and flexible solution for new terminals was the Over Rails Unloader, a diesel- or petrol-driven machine with an unloader bed that could be inserted beneath the hopper wagon but above track level, so that any siding with a fairly level hard surface alongside it could be used. Depots equipped with an Over Rails Unloader included Mossend, Oxford Hinksey and Bow.

Financial assistance for permanent coal handling facilities was available through the Government Section 8 Grant scheme, from which the depots at Ashford, Hove and Letchworth all benefited. However, the often unpredictable pattern of domestic coal flows made it difficult for potential customers to make a successful Section 8 application.

●

In its first year Speedlink Coal was hailed a success: it managed to maintain a constant volume by increasing its share of a declining market. BR even talked of setting up new terminals and services, such as a railhead in the East Midlands for receiving Welsh anthracite. But in reality the market declined too quickly for BR to maintain its volumes in the long term. One by one, the depots closed as the costs of serving them became prohibitive.

By the end of 1990 all domestic coal depots on the Southern Region had closed, together with Neasden, Ipswich, Broxbourne, Bishops Stortford, Cambridge, Peterborough, Aylesbury, Oxford, Swansea, Bordesley and Chadderton. The network pulled out of Healey Mills yard; most of its services were diverted to and from Doncaster, while Preston and Blackburn were now served from Washwood Heath. BR simplified the South Wales operations by withdrawing from Radyr and Pantyffynnon and concentrating all services on East Usk yard. Bucking the trend of closures was

Letchworth coal depot received a Section 8 grant so that it could join the Speedlink Coal network; unfortunately the traffic did not last long. No 31429 couples up to three empty HEAs from Letchworth on 23 March 1990, ready to continue its journey as 6M03, the 0325 from Temple Mills to Toton. The depot closed a few weeks later.

Birkenhead, which justified its own Speedlink Coal connection from Washwood Heath from early 1989, and Yeovil Junction, a new coal receiving depot that opened in 1988.

Ironically, the Speedlink Coal operation – renamed Network Coal to reinforce the separation from Speedlink – was to outlive the demise of BR's Speedlink network in July 1991. However, the overall volume of domestic coal traffic sank from 1.4 million tonnes in 1985/86 to 200,000 tonnes in 1992/93, with revenue plummeting from £12.5 million to £1.8 million in the same period. By that time the only remaining forwarding points were three locations in South Wales, and the only timetabled Network Coal service operated from East Usk yard to West Drayton. Residual traffic to Shrewsbury, Gobowen, Preston, Blackburn, Carlisle, Pensnett, Yeovil, Padworth, Bicester and Bow was carried by special trains as required.

BR therefore decided to abandon Network Coal with effect from April 1993. It would continue to serve just two distribution depots – West Drayton and Preston Deepdale – by running a daily block train to either depot, originating at Gwaun-cae-Gurwen, Onllwyn or Coedbach as required.

●

However, that was not quite the end of the story. The pre-privatisation companies Transrail and Loadhaul were willing to re-enter the domestic coal market and saw opportunities on a number of routes. In 1995 Transrail secured a contract with British Fuels to move containerised coal from a new coal preparation plant at Gascoigne Wood to Mossend, Aberdeen, Elgin and Inverness, with the trunk working routed via the Settle to Carlisle line and connections within Scotland provided by Enterprise wagonload services. Some containers were also delivered to Wick and Thurso. For the Scottish traffic British Fuels acquired 120

Electrically hauled coal trains were never a common sight on the West Coast Main Line. A Class 86 and Class 87 pairing, led by 'electric blue'-liveried No 86426, passes Galgate with 6S60, the 0900 Saturdays-only service from Coedbach to Mossend, on 15 April 1989.

Until 1983, the Settle to Carlisle line saw northbound coal movements from Yorkshire to Scotland. On 20 July 1982 No 40196 passes Settle Junction with the 6M64 wagonload service from Healey Mills to Carlisle, conveying mainly MCV mineral wagons. Just over a decade later, the route was carrying coal again – but now in the opposite direction from Ayrshire to English power stations.

redundant Cawoods containers and repainted them into its striking red livery.

Transrail used its Enterprise network to carry industrial coal from Coedbach to Mossend, containerised domestic coal from Coedbach to Seaforth, and, on a trial basis, industrial coal from Killoch to Keith. It also ran trainloads of hopper wagons from Killoch to Blackburn King Street and re-instated rail-borne deliveries of coal to Gobowen and Carlisle London Road. However, the service from South Wales to Preston Deepdale ceased in 1994.

Loadhaul did not attempt to recreate a wagonload network but was still able to carry out trial movements of domestic coal. In 1995 it moved coal in containers from Rossington to Mossend and Aberdeen, using its timetabled service from Tyne Yard to Inverurie, which normally carried agricultural lime. Loadhaul also carried coal in HEA hoppers to Llandudno Junction coal depot, which had been disused for several years.

Under EWS management, further gains and losses took place as the market for domestic coal continued its inexorable decline. In 1996 the company started moving a weekly train of anthracite from Onllwyn to Hull, using 30-foot Russells containers on FPA wagons that had been displaced by mgr hoppers on services to Coal Products Limited at Immingham. EWS also moved industrial coal in HEA hopper wagons from South Wales and Avonmouth to a distribution terminal at Doncaster Belmont, opened in 1995. On the debit side, West Drayton coal concentration depot finally closed in 1998.

The Smallshaws depot at Gobowen continued to receive occasional deliveries from various locations including Gascoigne Wood, Avonmouth and Daw Mill, while the company's other depot at

Shrewsbury New Yard also started receiving coal by rail, including a short-term contract to supply Ironbridge power station with coal from Millerhill in 1997. The Central Ordnance Depot at Bicester received seasonal trainloads of coal from Daw Mill in HEA hoppers. A surprising development in 1997/98 was the movement of bagged and palletised coal in railway-owned vans: several rafts of VDAs ran from the newly re-opened Tower colliery to St Blazey, and there was also a trial delivery to Fort William.

EWS moved containerised coal on a number of routes, using both 20-foot and 30-foot containers. The weekly British Fuels train from Gascoigne Wood to Mossend was withdrawn in 2000, but EWS continued to carry some Scottish traffic on scheduled Enterprise trains until 2003. The traffic from South Wales included deliveries in Russells containers to Ely, Hull, Gartcosh and Deanside as

The run-down of domestic coal traffic made large numbers of HEA hopper wagons redundant. Some were transferred to other traffic, including trainloads of coke from Redcar to Scunthorpe. No 56113 passes Stainforth & Hatfield with 6G45, the 1825 Scunthorpe to Tees Yard coke empties, on 29 May 1998. By early 2006 this flow provided the only regular work for the remaining fleet of HEA wagons.

well as three 'spot load' movements in former Cawoods containers to Falmouth Docks. The Ely and Deanside flows were still operating in 2005.

The Cawoods traffic to Northern Ireland dwindled, despite the awarding of an £82,000 Freight Facilities Grant in 2001 towards the refurbishment of 81 of the firm's containers. Trains ran to Seaforth container terminal from various loading points including Gascoigne Wood, Clipstone, Welbeck and Daw Mill, but finished in late 2004.

Appendix 1

Coal depots in England and Wales, 1983

S = depots to be retained for Speedlink
S? = depots possibly to be retained for Speedlink
Other depots to be closed

Aberdare	
Aberystwyth	
Abingdon	
Ammanford	
Ardwick West	S
Ashford	S
Aylesbury	S
Banbury	
Bangor	
Barking Ripple Lane	S?
Barrow-in-Furness (2 depots)	
Barrow-in-Furness (BFC)	S
Barry	
Beckenham Junction	S
Bedford	
Beverley	
Bicester	
Birkenhead North	S
Birtley	
Bishops Stortford	S
Blackburn King Street	S
Blackpool	S?
Blaenau Ffestiniog	
Blaydon	
Boston	
Bow	S?
Bradford Springmill Street	

Brentford Town	S?
Bridgend	
Bridlington	
Brigg	
Bristol Wapping Wharf	S
Brotton	
Broxbourne	S
Burnley	
Bury St Edmunds	
Buxton South	
Caerphilly	
Cambridge Brooklands	S
Cambridge Sleaford Street	
Canterbury West	
Cardiff Gabalfa	
Cardiff Roath	
Carlin How	
Carlisle London Road	S
Carmarthen	
Chadderton	S
Cheltenham	S
Chessington South	S
Chesterfield	
Chichester	
Colchester Hythe (2 depots)	S
Consett	
Corby	
Coventry	
Crewe	
Darlington Hope Town	
Deepcar	
Derby St Marys	
Dereham	
Dewsbury Railway Street	

Didcot	
Diss	
Driffield	
Droitwich Spa	S?
Durham	
Eastbourne	
Edge Hill	S
Exmouth Junction	S
Farnborough	
Felin Fran	
Filton Junction	S
Finchley Road	
Fishguard	
Fratton	S
Gaerwen	
Garforth	
Gateshead	
Gobowen	S
Goole Town	
Gorseinon	
Grangetown	
Grays	
Grimsby Holles Street	
Grimsby Railway Street	S
Grindleford	
Guide Bridge	
Haltwhistle	
Hamworthy	
Harrogate	
Hartlepool	
Haverfordwest	
Heaton (Newcastle)	
Hexham	
High Wycombe	
Hove	S
Huddersfield Hillhouse	

Hull Calvert Lane	S
Hull Sculcoates	S
Ipswich Derby Road	S
Jarrow	
Kidderminster	
Kidsgrove	
Kings Lynn Docks	
Knottingley	
Leamington Spa	
Leeds Balm Road	
Leicester Braunstone Gate	
Letchworth	S
Lincoln East	S
Lincoln Holmes	
Llandeilo	
Llandovery	
Llandudno Junction	S
Llanelli	
Llantrisant	
Lowestoft	S?
Luton Limbury Road	S
Machynlleth	
Maidstone West	
Malton	
Manor Park	S?
March	
Melton	
Middlesbrough	
Milford Haven	
Neasden	S
Neath	
Newark Castle	
Newbury	
Newcastle Forth	
Newcastle Victoria	

Newhaven	Preston Deepdale S	Southend Victoria S	Upton Park
Newport Dock Street S	Purley S	Sowerby Bridge	Valley
Northallerton	Reading Central	Spalding	Wadsley Bridge
Northampton	Rhyl	St Austell S?	Watford North S
Norwich Victoria S	Rhymney	St Neots	Wellington
Oxford Rewley Road	Rugby	Stainforth	Welshpool
Oxford South S	Salisbury	Stamford	West Drayton S
Padworth S	Saltburn	Stockport Edgeley	Whitby
Palace Gates S	Scarborough	Stockton North Shore	Whitland
Pembrey	Seamer	Stockton South	Wisbech
Pensnett S	Selby	Stonehouse S?	Wolverhampton
Penzance S?	Sheepbridge	Stratford Market	Worcester
Peterborough Crescent	Shildon	Strood S	Workington
Wharf S	Shrewsbury S	Sunderland (3 depots)	Wrexham
Peterborough South	Sleights	Swansea Eastern Depot S	Yarmouth
Plaistow	Small Heath S	Taplow	York Foss Islands
Plumstead S	South Lynn S?	Tolworth S	
Poole	Southampton Dibles	Tweedmouth S?	
Port Talbot	Wharf S	Tywyn	

Appendix 2

Coal statistics

UK coal production and consumption, million ton(ne)s				
Year	Production (deep mined)	Production (opencast)	Production (total)	Consumption
1960	189	8	197	200
1970	137	8	145	151
1980	110	13	123	120
1990	78	17	95	108
1998	28	16	44	62
2003	16	13	29	60

UK deep mines

Year	No of mines
1960	698
1970	293
1980	211
1990	65
2000	17
2004	9

Power stations with merry-go-round coal discharge, 1971

Fiddlers Ferry	CEGB
Blyth	CEGB
Ferrybridge 'C'	CEGB
Eggborough	CEGB
Thorpe Marsh	CEGB
Cottam	CEGB
West Burton	CEGB
High Marnham	CEGB
Staythorpe	CEGB
Ratcliffe	CEGB
Willington	CEGB
Drakelow 'C'	CEGB
Ironbridge 'B'	CEGB
Rugeley 'B'	CEGB
Didcot	CEGB
Aberthaw 'B'	CEGB
Cockenzie	SSEB
Longannet	SSEB

CEGB = Central Electricity Generating Board
SSEB = South of Scotland Electricity Board

UK deep mines, 2005

Mine	Annual output, million tonnes
Kellingley	0.9
Rossington	0.6
Harworth	0.9
Maltby	1.4
Thoresby	1.1
Welbeck	0.9
Daw Mill	3.0
Tower	0.5

Rail-borne coal traffic, million tonnes

Year	Total
1967	124
1972	89
1977	94
1986-87	77
1994-95	43
2003-04	42
2004-05	52

Rail-borne coal traffic, billion net tonne-kilometres

Year	Total
1986-87	5.0
1987-88	4.6
1988-89	4.8
1989-90	4.6
1990-91	5.0
1991-92	5.0
1992-93	5.4
1993-94	3.9
1994-95	3.3
1995-96	3.6
1996-97	3.9
1997-98	4.4
1998-99	4.5
1999-00	4.8
2000-01	4.8
2001-02	6.2
2002-03	5.7
2003-04	5.8
2004-05	7.0

Power stations receiving coal by rail, 2005

Power station	Owner	Capacity in MW
Fiddlers Ferry	Scottish & Southern Energy plc	2000
Lynemouth	Alcan	420
Wilton	ICI	100
Ferrybridge 'C'	Scottish & Southern Energy plc	2000
Eggborough	British Energy	2000
Drax	Drax Power Limited	4000
Cottam	EDF Energy	2000
West Burton	EDF Energy	2000
Ratcliffe	PowerGen	2000
Ironbridge 'B'	PowerGen	1000
Rugeley 'B'	International Power	1000
Didcot 'A'	RWE Npower	2000
Uskmouth	Uskmouth Power Company Ltd	1500
Aberthaw 'B'	RWE Npower	1500
Cockenzie	Scottish Power	1200
Longannet	Scottish Power	2400

Index